FREEDOM AND POSSIBILITY

FREEDOM
AND
POSSIBILITY

GOD RECONSIDERED

BERNARD P. PRUSAK

Paulist Press
New York / Mahwah, NJ

Cover image by monicore/Pixabay.com
Cover design by Joe Gallagher
Book design by Lynn Else

Library of Congress Cataloging-in-Publication Data
Names: Prusak, Bernard P., author.
Title: Freedom and possibility : God reconsidered / Bernard P. Prusak.
Description: New York/Mahwah, NJ : Paulist Press, [2023] | Includes index. | Summary: "The book considers the ongoing adventure of God acting through the randomness and chance of the evolutionary process"—Provided by publisher.
Identifiers: LCCN 2022057420 (print) | LCCN 2022057421 (ebook) | ISBN 9780809156351 (paperback) | ISBN 9780809187973 (ebook)
Subjects: LCSH: Human evolution—Religious aspects—Catholic Church. | Free will and determinism—Religious aspects—Catholic Church.
Classification: LCC BT712 .P78 2023 (print) | LCC BT712 (ebook) | DDC 231.7/652—dc23/eng/20230316
LC record available at https://lccn.loc.gov/2022057420
LC ebook record available at https://lccn.loc.gov/2022057421

ISBN 978-0-8091-5635-1 (paperback)
ISBN 978-0-8091-8797-3 (e-book)

Published by Paulist Press
997 Macarthur Boulevard
Mahwah, New Jersey 07430
www.paulistpress.com

Printed and bound in the
United States of America

To my granddaughters
Emma, Helena, Zoe, Anna Mary

CONTENTS

CONTENTS

Contents

PREFACE

THE UNIVERSE CAME INTO existence about thirteen billion, eight hundred million years ago. *Homo Sapiens* came into existence sometime before 200,000 years ago, or about 13,799,800,000 years after the beginning. God's plan unfolds over a vast evolutionary timeframe. When, and how, does one come to know what is really God's will and plan? As we shall see in the following pages, some Christians have thought it was God's will that women be submissive to men. Slavery was *not* said to be intrinsically evil by the Catholic Church until the twentieth century. In medieval times, heretics were burned at the stake. The Second Vatican Council declared that persons retain their right to religious freedom even if they are judged to be in error (*Dignitatis Humanae* 2). God patiently waits for humans to realize which perspectives and practices were really *not* what God willed or planned. As Kenan Osborne remarked, certain presentations of God are losing credibility in this day and age. An unreflected view of God "continues to bolster paternalistic and patriarchal elements of a given church community" or "self-assuredly explains God's plans and intentions for creation and redemption in intricate detail."[1] Such views of God and of God's will and plan need reconsideration.

Edward Schillebeeckx indicated that, for God, "history is an adventure, an open history [of free choices] for and of men and women…ultimately the world will be the expression of God's will in a way which is still not true and is now even contradicted by empirical experiences. So at this point we can never identify God's will in detail. One of the basic mistakes made by some of those who believe in God is to pretend that they know in detail what is 'the will of God' here and now."[2]

Humans often declare God's will in a way that is captive to past cultures, whereas God's will waits for humans to realize what should be. The last of the Decalogue (Ten Words) or Ten Commandments in Exodus 20:17 states, "You shall not covet your neighbor's house; you shall not covet your neighbor's wife, or male or female slave, or ox, or donkey, or anything that belongs to your neighbor." As the Second Vatican Council's Constitution on Revelation declares, "The words of God, expressed in human language, have been made like human discourse."[3] God's word comes to us in human, time-conditioned language. The male-dominated culture of the time, not God, considered a wife as property. But some did come to see a need to change that wording. In the seventh century BCE, Deuteronomy 5:21 instead said, "Neither shall you covet your neighbor's wife. Neither shall you desire your neighbor's house, or field, or male or female slave, or ox, or donkey, or anything that belongs to your neighbor." As Raymond Brown asked, "Are [the words] human formulations of a less specified revelation of divine moral demand?"[4]

Some past formulations of "God's will" call for reconsideration in new times. God's will is not necessarily what humans have declared it to be in a particular cultural moment. God's plan is not primarily what has been but, rather, what might become. God looks beyond what has been or is, to what is not yet.

ACKNOWLEDGMENTS

BRINGING A MANUSCRIPT to publication involves much dedicated work. I am grateful to Donna M. Crilly, the Senior Academic Editor at Paulist Press, for her efforts on my behalf. I also thank the entire production team at Paulist Press, particularly Joe Gallagher, the designer of the cover for this book.

1

CREATIVE FREEDOM
CREATING OTHER
FREEDOMS

THE BIBLE BEGINS with two creation narratives, placed side by side in the Book of Genesis. Genesis 2:4–24 is the earlier account, from about 950 BCE. It tells of God personally making the earth and the heavens, at a time when there were no bushes or plants in the field, since the LORD God (YHWH) had not yet made it rain. There was no human or earthling, *adam*, to till the soil, *adama*. A spring welled up from the ground and watered the surface of the soil. Then, like a potter, God (named YHWH) fashioned the human, *adam*, from the dust of the soil, *adama*, and blew the breath of life into his nostrils. The earthling or human whom God had fashioned was placed into a garden planted in Eden, to the east. The tree of life and the tree of the knowledge of good and evil were said to be there, amid many other prolific trees. And God is said to have commanded the human, "You may freely eat of every tree of the garden; but of the tree of the knowledge of good and evil you shall not eat, for in the day that you eat of it you shall die." God then formed, again from the soil, every animal on the ground and bird in the sky. Finally, since there was as yet no suitable, equal helper or partner for the human, *adam*, God took a rib from the human and built it into a woman (Gen 2:18–22). And the human said, "This, at last, bone of my bones and flesh of my flesh; this one shall be called Woman [*ishshah*], for out of Man [*ish*] this one was taken" (Gen 2:23). "Therefore a man leaves his father and his mother and clings to his wife, and they become one flesh. And the man and his wife were both naked, and were not ashamed (2:24–25).

The narrative continues. In chapter 3 a crafty serpent asks the woman whether God said that they should not eat from any tree in the garden. She responds, "We may eat of the fruit of the trees in the garden; but God said, 'You shall not eat of the tree that is in the middle of the garden, nor shall you touch it, or you shall die.'" The serpent replies, "You will not die; for God knows that when you eat of it your eyes will be opened, and you will be like God." Seeing the tree as good for food, and delightful to behold, the woman ate its fruit, and gave it to her husband to eat. Their eyes were opened; they saw that they were naked and made loincloths of fig leaves to cover themselves. Shame and guilt had emerged.

God, said to be walking in the garden, discovers the humans hiding and asks why they have covered themselves. Have they eaten from the tree of the knowledge of good and evil? The man says he ate because the woman gave him the fruit of the tree. The woman says the serpent tricked her and she ate. (The narrative reflects the patriarchal culture.) God curses the serpent so that it henceforth crawls on the ground. The woman is told she will suffer the pains of childbirth and be ruled by her husband. The man is told he will work the earth, toiling by the sweat of his brow, until he returns to the dust out of which he was taken. God stations a mythical guard, with a flaming, whirling sword, to block access to the tree of life.

The core of the narrative proclaims that a personal God is the creator of the world and everything in it, and humans are portrayed as having a relationship with God. The human capacity to make free decisions is imaginatively presented by means of the symbolic tree of the knowledge of good and evil. In this account, God shows little patience regarding human freedom, harshly reacting to the first free decision of disobedience. The narrative goes on to acknowledge that there will be many more evil decisions. It tells of a brother, Cain, a farmer, killing his brother Abel, a shepherd. Evil will intensify. Even a destructive flood, which God is said to send, and then to regret, will not wipe out evil.

Four or five centuries intervened before the other creation narrative in the first chapter of Genesis was composed. With the death of Solomon in 931 BCE, the kingdom that David had united was divided into two: Israel in the north and Judah in the south. The Assyrians invaded the Northern Kingdom in 722 BCE and dispersed its population in a way that destroyed their communal identity. Then, about 597, the Babylonians invaded the Southern Kingdom of Judah, destroyed Jerusalem and its temple, and deported its more prominent inhabitants into captivity in Babylon. That Babylonian exile ended about 538, when Cyrus, king of the Persians, conquered Babylonia and allowed the captive Jews to return to their native land.

During or soon after the Babylonian exile, Jewish priests, using the concept of a seven-day week developed by the Babylonians,[1] composed the account that describes God creating over six days and then resting on the seventh day. The narrative portrays God *as a personal thinker who speaks thoughts into existence*: "Let there be…" On each day, God simply spoke, and the words God said materialized. Likewise, on each day, God saw that what had come into existence "was good." On "day one," which we call Sunday, God said, "Let there be light." Light was separated from darkness, and God called the light day and the darkness night. On the second day, God spoke and a dome separated the waters above it from the waters below it. God called the dome heaven or sky. On the third day, God spoke and the waters under the sky were separated and dry land appeared. Plants and trees then grew on the land. On the fourth day, God spoke and lights emerged in the dome of the sky: the sun, moon, and stars. On the fifth day, God spoke and living creatures appeared in the sea and sky. On the sixth day, God spoke and animals emerged on earth, and finally the human, male and female, in God's image. Now seeing everything that had been made, God saw that it was *very* good. On the seventh day, God ceased working and rested from all the work of creation. God blessed and sanctified that day. The narrative's emphasis on the serene way that God created and the good that God saw in creation dramatically differed from the conflict between the gods portrayed in the Babylonian creation epic, *Enuma Elish*. Written on *seven* clay tablets, it told of a peace imposed and a creation accomplished by a god, Marduk, wielding a mighty sword. By contrast, the priestly creation account in Genesis conveys a peaceful tranquility.

Humans are said to have been created after all the animals on the sixth day and were thus not eyewitnesses to God's work of creating. That is likewise the case for the authors of the narrative. Their account declares the essential belief that God brought everything into existence. But their description of events comes from humans imagining how it happened. As Raymond Brown observed, the Bible is the human, time-conditioned, Word of God. "The fact that the 'word' of the Bible is human and time-conditioned makes it no less 'of God.'" In the Bible, God communicates self to the extraordinary extent that one can say that there is something "of God" in the words. "All other works, patristic, Thomistic, and ecclesiastic, are words *about* God; only the Bible is the word *of* God."[2] In reading the creation account, one may ask what is from God and what comes from the imaginative presentation of the authors.

In his *Literal Meaning of Genesis*, Augustine long ago noted inconsistencies in the creation narrative of the first chapter of Genesis. For example, God said, "Let there be light" and then called the light day and the darkness night on day one, before creating the sun, moon, and stars on the fourth day. There was no reference to God's creating the earth and water. They already seem to exist. The complexity of resolving such issues led Augustine sagely to emphasize the need for prudent scriptural interpretation. He offered advice that remains valid today:

Usually, even a non-Christian knows something about the earth, the heavens, and the other elements of this world, about the motion and orbit of the stars and even their size and relative positions, about the predictable eclipses of the sun and moon, the cycles of the years and the seasons, about the kinds of animals, shrubs, stones, and so forth, and this knowledge he holds to as being certain from reason and experience....If they find a Christian mistaken in a field which they themselves know well and hear him maintaining his foolish opinions about our books, how are they going to believe those books in matters concerning the resurrection of the dead, the hope of eternal life, and the kingdom of heaven, when they think their pages are full of falsehoods on facts which they themselves have learnt from experience and the light of reason? Reckless and incompetent expounders of Holy Scripture bring untold trouble and sorrow on their wiser brethren when they are caught in one of their mischievous false opinions and are taken to task....For then, to defend their utterly foolish and obviously untrue statements, they will try to call upon Holy Scripture for proof and even recite from memory many passages which they think support their position, although "they understand neither what they say nor the things about which they make assertion."[3]

Unfortunately, Augustine sometimes failed to heed his own caveats about interpreting Genesis. Later, in his *City of God*, he disputed the myth of the "antipodes," which claimed that humans inhabited the far side of the earth, deemed to be a globe suspended within the sphere of the heavens.[4] The sun was said to rise there when it sets for us, and the soles of the antipodes walking on the other side of the earth are opposite to our soles. Augustine considered the notion of human life in the opposite hemisphere to be a far-fetched assumption for which there was no evidence. Referring to "the waters that were gathered together" and called seas in Genesis 1:10, he declared that, even if one believed that the earth is a sphere, it did not follow that there was any land not covered by seas on the far side of the globe. Furthermore, he claimed that it was ludicrous to presume that persons from his side of the world could have sailed across the immense ocean and then populated the far side of the earth with humans descended from the one first man who fathered all humans. In Augustine's worldview, there had not been enough time for that to have happened.

The biblical creation narratives were composed about 13,799,997,000 years after the beginning of the universe. But creation has never remained a story told once and for all. Since its beginnings, the narrative has been rethought and renewed. The Fourth Gospel, attributed to John, offered a retelling of Genesis 1 that identified Jesus with the preexistent Word through whom everything was created: "In the beginning was the Word, and the Word was with [the] God and the Word was God. He was in the beginning with [the] God. All things came into being through him, and without him not one thing came into being....And the Word became flesh and lived among us" (John 1:1–3, 14).[5] "All things have been created through him and for him" (Col 1:16). "Long ago God spoke to our ancestors in many and various ways by the prophets, but in these last days he has spoken to us by a Son, whom he appointed heir of all things, through whom he also created the worlds [aiōnas: literally, eons, containing the material universe]" (Heb 1:1–2).

GROWING UNDERSTANDING OF THE WORLD, THE UNIVERSE, AND GOD

Humans have not always thought about themselves and the world in exactly the same way. Nor have they always thought about God in the same way, or even used that kind of term. The Bible tells of a relationship offered by the absolute mystery that we call "God," and speaks of the profound meaning and purpose of human life. Prehistoric humans may have intuited, in an unformulated manner, that there was a deeper reality beyond what they experienced in everyday existence. God "is the final word before we become silent, the word which allows all the individual things we can name to disappear into the background, the word in which we are dealing with the totality which grounds them all."[6]

Greco-Roman culture upheld an earth-centered universe. Plato envisioned the universe as a perfect sphere with the earth fixed in its center.[7] All the planets and stars rotated around the earth at uniform speed in perfect circles. For Plato, such mathematically precise and unvarying circular motion is an activity of intelligent heavenly bodies that participate in the order of Being, and is therefore the visible, material embodiment of the unmoving perfection of a purely intelligible order, the realm of the Ideas. The most transcendent Idea, "the Good," is self-contained, pure being, approachable only through contemplation. It excludes all nonbeing, limitation, and the imperfection of becoming.[8] Aristotle likewise conceived of a stationary earth that was surrounded by stars attached to concentric, transparent spheres, like the layers of an onion. Change or incomplete motion existed only inside the sphere of the moon. Outside that sphere, the heavens were said to be eternal and unalterable. The fixed stars moved in perfect circles, at unvarying speeds, considered to be the only complete or perfect motion. Beyond the outermost sphere of stars was the realm of the absolutely unmoved (*apathēs*) Prime Mover.[9]

The insights of Nicolaus Copernicus (1473–1543) and Galileo Galilei (1564–1642) removed the earth from the center of the universe. Johannes Kepler (1571–1630) discovered that the motion of the planetary bodies is elliptical and not perfectly circular. The insights of Isaac Newton (1642–1727) regarding gravity and the tendency of bodies in motion to stay in motion explained why orbits were elliptical. That eliminated the need for Aristotle's First Mover who, as a Final Cause, produced the circular motion of the intelligent outermost sphere.

Further significant insights followed. *On the Origin of Species by Means of Natural Selection, or the Preservation of Favoured Races in the Struggle for Life*, published in 1859 by Charles Darwin (1809–82), proposed a theory of natural selection and evolution—establishing the idea that living organisms emerged through a process of natural development. Darwin's perspectives were later related to the laws of heredity of Gregor Mendel, OSA (1822–84), that became known and accepted only after 1900. The theories of relativity proposed by Albert Einstein (1879–1955) introduced new ways of seeing the relationship between matter and energy, space and time. Max Planck (1858–1947), Nils Bohr (1885–1962), Werner Heisenberg (1901–76), and many others established quantum mechanics to study the world of the infinitesimally small, seventeen subatomic particles, such as quarks, gluons, Higgs boson particles, fermions, and muons. Today, sophisticated telescopes capture images coming to us from occurrences in the far distant past, traveling toward us at the speed of light through the once inconceivable vastness of the universe. We have begun to put the universe into our heads in a way that far exceeds the capacity of humans in the past.

Because the human story remains a work in progress, the same is true of the Christian narrative. Our growing scientific understanding of the world and universe can enable a deeper understanding of the ultimate mysterious presence that we call God. In Darwin's time, many so-called deists maintained that God had created things at the beginning, but was no longer actively involved in creation. But evolution helps us to understand that creation is an ongoing project for God.[10] It is nothing like building a car, a watch, a washing machine, or a woman from a rib! As the young Joseph Ratzinger, who would become Pope Benedict XVI, declared, "The model from which creation must be understood is not the craftsman but the creative mind, creative thinking…a creative freedom that creates further freedoms. To this extent one could very well describe Christianity as a philosophy of freedom."

The creative thinking that is the ground of all being is truly conscious thinking that both knows and loves: "it is creative because it is love…because it can love as well as think, it has given its thought the freedom of its own existence, objectivized it, released it into distinct being….This thinking knows its thought in its distinct being, loves it and, loving, upholds it….[If] the being that upholds and encompasses everything, is consciousness, freedom, and love, then it follows automatically that the supreme factor in the world is not cosmic necessity but freedom….This leads to the conclusion that freedom is evidently the necessary structure of the world."[11]

RETELLING THE CREATION NARRATIVE

Revelation does not involve words floating down from the sky. The Word of God is conveyed in human, time-conditioned words, via human experience of, and reflection on a profound personal relationship being offered. Communicating the essential message of God as Creator in our era can benefit from a retelling. God *as a personal thinker wills God's thoughts into existence through a process that unfolds over billions of years, rather than six days.*

In a vacant, empty darkness, without matter, space, or time, there were not yet quarks, protons or neutrons, atoms or molecules, and no galaxies, stars, planets, or moons. There was no past, present, or future, no before or after, up or down, left or right, forward or backward, no becoming, no birth or death. Before the beginning of time, there existed only a boundless personal consciousness, ever-thinking limitless possibility—envisioning all that was conceivable. That Thinker or Source, whom Jesus later called

Abba, was eternally begetting an infinite Expression of everything that was conceivable. And from the intimate relationship of Begetter and Expression, a Spirit of Love eternally proceeded. As Genesis 1:27 insightfully declares, the image of God is male *and* female. Three in One thought, expressed, and radiated infinite possibility and love. Because no *other* existed, the relational love of three in one had not yet been named. It was unknown by anyone and remained a Mystery that would be made known and, in English, called God.

The eternal communion of Three in One pulsated with a dynamic, personal energy—eternally thinking and expressing infinite possibility and love. Infinite power was suffused with intelligence, freedom, and love. The Relational Oneness of Thinker, Expression, and Love existed as an eternal fullness that needed nothing. Being omnipotent in love, Three in One freely chose to initiate a self-giving relationship. The eternal Expression of unlimited fullness and possibility communicated outward from Three in One: "Let there be...." A puff of energy was breathed into a previously vacant, empty darkness!

The universe was birthed as an incredibly hot, dense dot. That infinitesimal, newborn universe then expanded in a rapid burst of inflation. Within the first second, space inflated faster than the speed of light, doubling in size over ninety times, from subatomic size to the size of a golf ball. In the first minutes, quarks bonded to form protons and neutrons that combined to form the nuclei of hydrogen and helium. At three minutes, the newborn universe was an expanding and cooling fireball of hydrogen and helium nuclei. Time had begun, about 13.8 billion years ago, and within ten seconds, there would be photons and nucleosynthesis, light in the darkness. About 400,000 years later, the photons became cosmic microwave background radiation. The successive stages of the evolving universe would require long periods of time. It would take at least two hundred million more years for the first galaxies and stars to be born, out of huge clouds of hydrogen and helium being compressed by gravity. The gaseous fog of the early universe would gradually dissipate.

The universe developed in ways that were not totally predetermined. The evolutionary process had an internal, dynamic spontaneity, in which randomness and chance were blended with what came to be called the laws of nature. As hydrogen atoms bumped into one another, some inevitably united to form molecules. That process inevitably became ever more complex. The supernova explosions of large stars, among the first two generations of stars, spewed "stardust" out into the cosmos. That matter was then recycled by a third generation of stars. The star named Sun with its system of planets and moons began forming about 4.6 billion years ago from a molecular cloud of interstellar dust and hydrogen gas. In the course of that process, the heavier elements of carbon, nitrogen, and oxygen emerged. A billion years later, primitive forms of life emerged. Humans still seek to understand and explain the prebiotic chemistry that led to the formation of RNA and DNA.

There was a period of about three billion years between the appearance of primitive life forms on earth and the appearance of intelligent life. We may ask, "Why was this period not many times longer or many times shorter than the lifetime of the sun?... The life of the sun depends upon gravity, gas laws, thermonuclear reactions, and so forth. The development of intelligent beings [the human brain] relies upon chemistry and ultimately biology in an evolving universe where an interplay of chance and necessity do not allow a clear determination of time durations. Why is it that the evolution of human beings fits comfortably into the life of the sun?"[12]

The Relationship of Three in One was the quintessence of understanding and expression, freedom and love. The outward expression called creation launched a self-giving offer of relationship, which required that there be others who likewise had understanding, freedom, and the ability to love, in response to the offer of relationship. To that end, Three united in One initiated a process *wherein the possibility of freedom freely emerged from within*. The seeds of freedom and creativity were implanted into the process. In an intrinsic development over the course of billions of years, the process eventually became conscious and free from within, with the emergence of earthlings or terrestrials having brains with the capacity for reflective understanding and expression, and the profound freedom needed in order to love. Given that freedom, the possibility of hatred and violence also emerged. That was not what the Three united in One intended. The unconstrained freedom that made genuine love possible entailed that risk.

The term *Homo* is applied to various species that began to emerge over the course of the last two million years.[13] The earliest specimens of *Homo sapiens* within Africa are now dated to a time before 200,000 years ago.[14] The buried remains of *Homo sapiens* discovered in caves at Mount Carmel, dated between 100,000 and 80,000 years ago, indicate an early migration out of Africa.[15] Genetic evidence points to a later, major dispersal out of Africa into Asia and Europe, starting around 60,000 years ago. Those migrations gave rise to the populations presently existing on those continents.[16] Genetics also shows that there had been mating with those known as Neanderthal and Denisovan humans. Colonization in Europe occurred before 40,000 years ago, and in Australia before 30,000, perhaps even 50,000 years ago. Farming began about 10,000 years ago and laid the foundation for the subsequent rise of towns and eventually the civilizations that developed writing. Invoking biblical evidence, Augustine calculated that less than 6,000 years had passed since the origin of humans.[17] Actually, *Homo sapiens* had emerged and populated the far side of earth across the ocean long before that. Given such data, how should we think anew about God, and about ourselves?

SELF-TRANSCENDENCE WITHIN EVOLUTION: INTELLIGENCE AND FREEDOM

Evolution reveals an inbuilt capacity for self-transcendence. The matter of a lifeless universe produced life, and then life became a self-conscious embodied spirit.[18] Past Christian tradition spoke of God infusing souls into bodies. One might say that, with the emergence of humans, material evolution disclosed its innate, potential spirituality.[19] Chimpanzees have twenty-four pairs of chromosomes; humans have twenty-three pairs. A mutation found in chromosome number 2 caused two chromosomes to fuse into one, and something radically new emerged: the brain of *Homo sapiens*, with the capacity for self-reflective consciousness and language. In a faith perspective, that directionality is attributed to the creator of the evolutionary process that has become conscious and endowed with the capacity to be free—in and through the human intellect and volition. When the evolutionary process produced consciousness in and through the human brain, a spiritual dimension had emerged. Rather than a dualistic emphasis on body and soul, we might better say that a human is an embodied spirit. To know and love involves our physical brain. A human is a being in whom matter and spirit (soul) are essentially united.

Now, hundreds of thousands of years after our emergence, we humans more and more take the universe into our minds and explain the process by which we came into existence. Like much of the evolutionary process, a long period of development was required for that ability to come to fruition. Why did the kind of freedom that makes love possible emerge?

By theologically naming the self-organizing universe shaped by an evolutionary process "creation," we recognize God's initiative and commitment, both in its origin and in its ongoing development. God, who is the personification of freedom and love, willed that there be others with the personal freedom that makes love possible. As Edward Schillebeeckx observed, the emergence of humans with intelligence and freedom is "a sort of 'divine yielding,' making room for the other."[20] Giving creative space to human beings exercising freedom involves a kenotic self-limitation on God's part. It gives rise to a being independent of the omnipotence of the creator.[21] In *Gaudium et Spes* (36, 41, and 56), the Second Vatican Council acknowledged that God has endowed humans with a certain autonomy for shaping the world. One might say that God has entered into a partnership with humans as "created co-creators"—shapers of the evolutionary process from within.[22] Freely choosing to depend on the initiatives of human freedom, the God who is omnipotent in love freely chose to become vulnerable and defenseless, and undertook an adventure full of risks. As Ilia Delio put it, "God evolves the universe and brings it to its completion through the instrumentality of human beings."[23]

Yves Congar once wrote, "Perhaps the greatest disaster that has afflicted modern Catholicism was that in doctrine and catechetics it turned to God and religion 'as they are in themselves,' instead of ceaselessly enquiring at the same time what this all means for men and women."[24] It proclaimed a God without human beings and without a world. The chapters of this book present God as intimately involved. "God's world is bound up with our human world."[25]

And as Gabriel Daly notes,

This earthly life is shot through with salvific instances which demand to be recognized as such by faith. Grace is not an abstract or invisible entity granted by God directly and without mediation. It always coexists with tangible realities and is mediated by those realities. There is no such thing as a grace which is grace and nothing else. There are only graced persons, events, and things. If we wish to discover and encounter grace, we must turn to the created world, because it is the created world which supplies the materials and occasions that become the vehicles of grace.[26]

What is more, Three in One always planned a second divine expression outward. Thousands of years after the emergence of humans, the eternal, divine Word, which expressed "Let there be light" into the darkness, would become a participant in creation, revealing a divine way of being human and a human way of being divine, amid the brokenness of human history.

2

THE CREATOR OF FREEDOM DOES NOT DOMINATE OR RETALIATE

THE ORIGINS OF the Bible date to the period around 1000 BCE when the oral traditions of the twelve tribes of Israel began to be written down. That was followed by an extended process of compilation. The biblical period is thus about 3,000 years old. By contrast, modern humans evolved more than 200,000 years ago. We know relatively little about the first 200,000-plus years of human existence. The first modern humans, with their large brains, were radically open in their potential to know and to understand, but limited in the actualization of that ability. Human knowledge about ourselves and our world would grow by incremental steps over millennia. Early humans determined which foods were good to gather and eat. They reflected on the cycle of seasons and rainy periods and then calculated when particular crops should be planted. They domesticated horses, camels, donkeys, and dogs. They invented the wheel, tools, and weapons. They began to write only about 4,000 years ago. Early humans could watch birds flying in the sky, but the first human flights did not occur until Kitty Hawk in 1903. Once upon a time, the developments of the last century would have been unimaginable. Humans now take the universe into their minds and explain the process by which they came into existence. A long period of development was required for that ability to come to fruition.

The growing understanding of our world and the universe can positively refine our understanding of God, especially God's patience. In the third chapter of Genesis, God was portrayed as irritated by the fact that humans, exercising their freedom, had come to know not only good but also evil. He curses the serpent, tells the woman she will suffer the pains of childbirth and be ruled by her husband, and tells the man he will toil by the sweat of his brow, until he dies—which is ensured by blocking access to that figurative tree of life. That portrayal stands in stark contrast to the concept of a God who conceived and willed into existence an evolutionary process endowed with an internal integrity that unfolded over billions of years and ultimately gave rise to human consciousness and freedom. As the source of love, and of the underlying freedom that makes love possible, God would know that granting freedom was a risk. As Joseph Ratzinger noted, "a world created and willed on the risk of freedom and love" can be the playground of light and love or the arena of darkness and evil. "It accepts the mystery of darkness for the sake of the greater light constituted by freedom and love."[1] God's human partners can resist what they ought to decide or become, but God remains faithful to human freedom and does not retaliate.

ASSIGNING CAUSES FOR HISTORICAL EVENTS OR NATURAL CALAMITIES

Previous perspectives often presupposed an offended, retaliatory, punitive image of God. Jacques-Bénigne Bossuet's *Discourse on Universal History*, published in 1681, emphasized the need to trust that God is operative in the world's history even if one sees no sign of that. Carrying forward the template of Augustine's *City of God*, Bossuet found evidence of divine providence in the rise and fall of empires. Thus, for him, the French monarchy—linked to Charlemagne's establishment of a Christian empire—was heir to the Roman and Holy Roman empires. Divine intervention in human history was a given. Despite the intentions of those shaping history, the outcome is determined by God: "There is no human power which does not unintentionally serve other ends than its own. God alone can subject everything to his will. That is why every event is unexpected if we perceive only its specific causes; and yet the world goes forward in a foreordained sequence."[2] For Bossuet, conquerors "are for the most part merely instruments of divine vengeance...to chastise his children and to bring down his enemies."[3]

Voltaire's *Essay on the Manners and Mind of Nations, and on the Principal Facts of History from Charlemagne to Louis XIII*, published in 1756, began where Bossuet had ended—with Charlemagne—and intended to refute Bossuet's view of divine providence intervening in history. It focused on cultural, economic, and political history, without the theological framework emphasized by Bossuet. For Voltaire, God brought the world into existence but then withdrew from any relationship with it. God has no relationship with humans in history. Creation is divorced from any relationship with God.[4] That perspective would be termed *deism*. Bossuet and Voltaire thus represented a contradictory either/or: a God of total control versus a God who has absolutely no relationship to humanity and its history.

On November 1, 1755, the city of Lisbon was devastated by a powerful earthquake that killed thousands and destroyed two-thirds of the city. Since it occurred on the Feast of All Saints, many churches collapsed on the faithful assembled in them. The nature of the event generated profound reflection about divine providence, with some declaring the earthquake to be divine punishment for sin. By contrast, in the conclusion to *Candide*, published in 1759 and written with the earthquake in mind, one of Voltaire's characters suggests that humans are like the mice on a ship. His Majesty is not concerned about their comfort.[5]

In an essay published in 1756 and entitled "On the Causes of Earthquakes on the Occasion of the Calamity that Befell the Western Countries of Europe towards the End of Last Year," Immanuel Kant (1724–1804) presented a different perspective.[6] He maintained that earthquakes are the result of natural causes and in no way punishments sent by God. Kant engaged and applied a new, scientific way of thinking that had been emerging. He sought to show that earthquakes have purely physical causes, attributing them to the collapse of huge, empty cavities under the earth due to the effects of various kinds of vapors. Rather than fearing earthquakes and considering them as punishments sent by God, Kant advocated efforts to control their effects. He correctly assigned physical causes for earthquakes, but the wrong kind. Alfred Wegener proposed the theory of "continental drift" in 1915. A fuller understanding of plate tectonics and faults emerged in the 1950s and '60s through studies of the earth's magnetic field.

HUMAN HISTORY IS NOT PREDETERMINED

As John Polkinghorne has noted, we live in a world of dynamic systems reflecting a "structured randomness."[7] An intrinsic indeterminism in the overall order enables an envelope of possibility and the openness of the future to the new.[8] There is an innate creativity in virtue of which the new continuously emerges through the interplay of law and chance. The potentialities of this universe would go unactualized without chance. God does not soak up the freedom of the open process: "freedom is given to the whole cosmos to be and make itself."[9] The randomness and chance of the physical world prepare the way for human freedom: "there is no detailed blueprint, only a set of laws with an inbuilt facility for making interesting things happen."[10] Human creativity thus works within the gaps, or envelope, of possibility. God's action within this unpredictable open process will always be hidden, "though it may be discerned by faith."[11] "God is indeed in charge, but in such a way that our freedom, including our freedom to resist his intentions, forms part of the Creator's master-plan."[12] God's involvement with the becoming of the world within time is inseparable from the eternal aspect of the divine nature: "for God is not in thrall to the flux of becoming, only in intimate and interacting relationship with it."[13]

Emphasizing the future of creation and God's continuing activity in it, Jürgen Moltmann speaks of God as open to the world and the world as open to God, "the Foundation who enables all potentiality."[14] Polkinghorne speaks of a world of true becoming, released from physical determinism and "open to both bottom-up and top-down causality."[15] As D. J. Bartholomew emphasizes, "Only in a world with a sufficient degree of randomness is there enough flexibility to combine a broadly determined line of development with adequate room for the exercise of real freedom on the part of individuals."[16] That "allows us to maintain at one and the same time that God determines the end and the lawfulness of the macro-universe and that there is indeterminism on the micro-scale."[17] Arthur Peacocke holds that the mutual interplay of chance and law is creative, "for it is the combinations of the two which allows new forms to emerge and evolve."[18] As Creator, God is "an Improvisor of unsurpassed ingenuity."[19]

God has chosen vulnerably to depend on our responsible initiatives. As Schillebeeckx declares, "Christians must give up a perverse, unhealthy and inhuman doctrine of predestination....We must give up a world history laid down 'from eternity'....Nothing is determined in advance:...in the world of human activity there is the possibility of free choices."[20] God has chosen to depend on and work through the secondary causality of human freedom.[21] Women and men "are called to be conscious collaborators with God."[22]

To be free is to have to choose. But, as Alfred North Whitehead warned, "one must be careful not to simply identify the world with becoming and flux, and God with being and permanence."[23] The world might protect the present status quo, unless it were lured toward concretizing a new subject and ideal by an underlying energy of realization, which is creativity. For instance, many opposed the abolition of slavery or women's suffrage. Whitehead proposed that, as the "lure for feeling, the eternal urge of desire," God is the source of becoming who overcomes the world's compulsion with the static present by the persuasive lure of what might be.[24] Whitehead's perspective stands in need of further refinement.

Keith Ward has suggested thinking of the Spirit "as a cooperating influence for good, never obliterating the proper autonomy of nature, but conforming it, slowly but surely, to patterns laid down in the eternal Word."[25] More recently, Denis Edwards has proposed a theology that emphasizes the active influence of the Spirit as the power of becoming within history. God, acting through the Spirit in our midst, invites and enables creativity and self-transcendence—"enabling the new to emerge from within creation itself."[26] Ormond Rush calls for a new pneumatology "from below," which he terms a "reception pneumatology."[27] It links "the creative involvement of human beings in the decisions of history" with "the creative interpretation of 'what God would want.'"[28] "In response to the task given by our God, *it is up to us to work it out as we go along*—with the help of the Holy Spirit whispering through all the criteria for fidelity and continuity."[29] God's challenging and liberating power is inwardly present, seeking to draw humans to their deepest potentialities. What God wills may be creatively *becoming* rather than what was.

Having emerged in the evolutionary process, humans now shape that process on this planet. It has been placed into our care. Just as God, motivated by love, makes certain renunciations in bringing humans into existence, humans must now more and more ask how they should self-limit. For example, what human renunciations are necessary for the ecological health of our planet? What should geneticists do and *not* do, given that genetic modifications affect the future of evolution? There is a pressing need to exercise a responsible freedom, to preserve the ecosystem out of which we have emerged and on which we depend for our continued existence. In addition to the stockpiles of the other nuclear nations, the United States maintains about 10,000 nuclear weapons. As Gabriel Daly has noted, "In theological language sin enters creation through culture."[30] Greed and lust for power shape our world in ways that are threatening to both nature and humans.

Karl Rahner has emphasized that "humans attain their transcendental future, union with God, only by means of the material of this world and its history."[31] Shaping the future is a task given to humans. In that regard, we must be conscious collaborators "who listen to God in history."[32] The challenge to which we are now called involves the very salvation of the planet under our feet, as it revolves around a third-generation star within the wilderness of a vast universe. Love of the earth and its inhabitants must shape our efforts. We have nowhere else to go!

As Pope Francis declares, "God, who calls us to generous commitment and to give him our all, offers us the light and the strength needed to continue on our way. In the heart of this world, the Lord of life, who loves us so much, is always present. He does not abandon us, he does not leave us alone, for he has united himself definitively to our earth, and his love constantly impels us to find new ways forward. *Praise be to him*!" (*Laudato Si'* 245).

3

JESUS

God's Love Became a Defenseless Human Love

PRESUPPOSING THE "present-day evolutionary view of the world" and acknowledging the writings of Teilhard de Chardin, but proceeding without depending on Chardin's work, Karl Rahner wrote his reflections on "Christology within an Evolutionary View of the World" in the early 1960s. He noted that the "condition of mutual relatedness between spirit and matter is not simply a static condition, but has itself a history."[1] Emphasizing that "becoming *more*" as an active self-transcendence is a necessary notion in our thinking, Rahner declared that "man is...the self-transcendence of living matter."[2] The material cosmos becomes conscious of itself in the innumerable personal self-consciousnesses of corporeal humans.[3] Presupposing that the goal of the world consists in God communicating self to it, the dynamism of the world's becoming by self-transcendence is really the "first step towards this self-communication and its acceptance by the world."[4] "God's self-communication is...communication of freedom and inter-communication between the many cosmic subjectivities." It takes place historically in a way that involves time and space and requires a free decision of acceptance.[5] For humanity to be able to respond to God's self-giving relationship, freedom is essential. The ability to love presupposes freedom; love is the greatest exercise of freedom.

GOD ALWAYS INTENDED
TO BECOME HUMAN IN JESUS

Jesus, as a fully human participant in biological evolution and the natural history of the material cosmos, is God's unsurpassable self-communication and humanity's irrevocable, free acceptance of God's offer of relationship. In Jesus, the cosmos attains "the climax of development in which the world comes absolutely into its own presence and into the direct presence of God."[6] Rahner sees the incarnation as something God always intended, as the culmination of the divine plan of creation. It is not an afterthought in order to restore a divine world order contaminated by the sins of mankind.[7] Creation and the incarnation are not two disparate, juxtaposed acts but rather two moments and phases of the one process of God's self-renunciation and self-expression into what is other.[8] They are inseparable aspects of God's self-giving in relationship. Ilia Delia has shown how Rupert of Deutz in the twelfth century and especially Franciscan scholars of the thirteenth century John Duns Scotus and Bonaventure, who emphasized God's love, foreshadowed Rahner's perspective.[9]

From the beginning of creation onward, God is not an outsider to the world but intimately involved in it. As an ever present self-communicating divine mystery. God immanently sustains and is inwardly present within the ongoing process of the evolution of the universe, but without the need for intervention in its natural development. Nonintervention has not excluded *kenotic* or self-emptying involvement. In the incarnation, in and through Jesus, God became a participant in the evolutionary process, freely opening self to sharing in and being affected by the goodness and the brokenness of the world.[10] Jesus is both the unsurpassable divine self-communication and humanity's irrevocable response.

Jesus did not simply tell sinners and outcasts that God loved them and would be merciful to them. He invited persons whom others considered sinners and outcasts to eat and drink with him, for which he endured criticism and derision: "This fellow welcomes sinners and eats with them." He was called "a glutton and a drunk, a friend of tax collectors and sinners." Sharing meals with persons disdained by others powerfully proclaimed the reign of the merciful and loving *Abba* (Father) whom Jesus compared to a shepherd searching for a lost sheep, a woman searching for a lost coin, or a father running to welcome home his prodigal son. A celebratory meal followed![11] The offer of divine forgiveness came without preconditions. When Jesus invited himself to Zacchaeus's house, those who saw it murmured, "He has gone to be the guest of one who is a sinner," for Zacchaeus was the wealthy chief tax collector in Jericho. His unconditional acceptance by Jesus produced a remarkable transformation: "Look, half of my possessions, Lord, I will give to the poor; and if I have defrauded anyone of anything, I will pay back four times as much" (Luke 19:7–8).

GOD DID NOT REQUIRE OR WANT THE DEATH OF JESUS

Anselm wrote the *Cur Deus Homo* (*Why God Became Human*), in 1098, to counter a notion that Jesus's death was a ransom or price paid to Satan. Anselm instead maintained that the price had to be paid to God, since Adam and Eve had offended God and God's honor. Because God is infinite, Anselm declared Adam and Eve's offense was infinite. As finite creatures, they could not satisfy for an infinite offense. Out of mercy, God sent Jesus to satisfy for their offense. As divine, Jesus could satisfy for an infinite offense; as human, Jesus satisfied on behalf of humans. Being sinless, he did not have to die since death was considered a punishment for sin. By dying on the cross, he "more than infinitely satisfied" for humanity's offense.

The extreme penances that had been imposed for serious sins in earlier centuries were likely the foundation for Anselm's emphasis on satisfaction. He interpreted Jesus's death as a price that satisfied the debt owed for an infinite offense. That then became primary in western Christian thought. Contemporary theology stands closer to Peter Abelard's emphasis on the saving power of the love manifested in the passion and death of Christ: seeing Christ's love for us inspires us to love.[12] As Ratzinger declares, the cross "is the expression of the radical nature of the love that gives itself completely." God and Jesus, as God become fully human, are involved in a self-giving love. Jesus's death was not a satisfaction or a price paid to an offended God.[13]

God did not plan, intend, or want the crucifixion. The dark side of human freedom led those wielding power in Jerusalem to crucify Jesus. God, ever the guarantor of human freedom, did not intervene. As Psalm 22 on the lips of the dying Jesus (Mark 15:34; Matt 27:46) indicates, Jesus died in a dark night of faith, trusting that the God he called Abba was with him.[14] Despite the fact that humans killed Jesus, God saved humans through that event.[15] As Ratzinger emphasizes, "It is not [humans] who [go] to God with a compensatory gift, but God who comes to [humans]...."[16] "In Christ God was reconciling the world to himself" (2 Cor 5:19).

The death of Jesus on the cross was not a penalty or ransom price that God demanded. Quite the opposite, the vulnerable and defenseless death of Jesus on a cross was God's gift to humans: an act of self-giving love. God shared in the brokenness of the world. In and through Jesus, God participated in the struggle of this world and the hate-filled violence that the powerful inflict on those who are defenseless. In his life and death, Jesus manifested a divine way of being human and a human way of being divine. "God's transcendent overcoming of human failure is historically incorporated in Jesus' never-ceasing love for God and man, during and in the historical moment of his [seeming] failure on the cross."[17] As Gabriel Daly affirmed, "It was love which conceived the whole venture; and it was love which carried it through (the point which Abelard appreciated and expressed in his theory of the exemplary action of Christ). The love of God for his creation was definitively expressed in the love of Jesus for his Father and for his fellow human beings."[18]

GOD CHOSE TO SHARE THE HORROR OF INNOCENT SUFFERING

Jesus's death was not the payment of a debt owed or a satisfaction offered to God. Rather, it was a gift that God gave to us: "in Christ God was reconciling the world to himself" (2 Cor 5:19). In Jesus, God became a defenseless, innocent victim, so fully human that those who wielded power over society could crucify him. As Walter Kasper observes, "On the cross God's self-renouncing [*kenotic*] love is embodied with ultimate radicalness....The cross is the utmost that is possible to God in his self-surrendering love; it is 'that than which a greater cannot be thought'; it is the unsurpassable self-definition of God....Only an almighty love can give itself wholly to the other and be a helpless love."[19]

The God of Jesus Christ is not unmoved or *apathēs*, but is rather a God of "sym-pathy" or "com-passion," a God who *suffers with* humans. Because God is love, God freely chooses to be affected by those whom God loves. The suffering of God arises from a love that seeks to overcome suffering.[20] As Gabriel Daly declares, "God in Christ shares in the horror of innocent suffering."[21] God's voluntary self-limitation in endowing humans with freedom is inseparable from God's likewise choosing to be affected by what is happening in creation. In Jesus, God's love became a human love. Jesus died defenseless and vulnerable, nailed to a cross, but his free decision to love even those putting him to death actualized God's goal for creation: the freedom to love. God did not thwart the freedom of those who crucified Jesus, but God did have the final word. The resurrection reveals God's ultimate transformation and overcoming of suffering, and ratifies Jesus's "way" of being human.

4

FOUNDATIONAL (ORIGINAL) SIN

A Viral Freedom

DURING THE FIRST three centuries, baptism was not considered a washing away of "original sin." The concept did not yet exist. In his Epistle to the Romans (6:1–11), Paul proclaimed that all who have been baptized into Christ Jesus were baptized into his death. Being immersed in the water, they were buried with him into death. They then came out of the water united with the risen Christ. Their old, sinful self had died with Christ. Their new self was no longer enslaved to sin and lived with Christ in newness of life. The Gospel of John presents baptism as a rebirth: being born of water and the Spirit. Everyone who is thus "born from above" is born of the Spirit. "What is born of the Spirit is spirit" (John 3:6).

In his *First Apology*, written in Rome shortly after 150 CE, Justin Martyr referred to baptism as a new birth in which one is born again and illuminated: "This washing is called illumination, as those who learn these things are illuminated in the mind. And he who is illuminated is washed in the name of Jesus Christ, who was crucified under Pontius Pilate, and in the name of the Holy Spirit, who through the prophet foretold all the things about Jesus."[1]

The notion of "original sin" was conceived in the early fifth-century dispute between Augustine and Pelagius regarding the nature of human freedom. Their positions involved divergent interpretations of a Latin translation of Romans 5:12: *propter ea sicut per unum hominem in hunc mundum peccatum intravit et per peccatum mors, et ita in omnes homines mors pertransiit in quo omnes peccaverunt.* Pelagius read the passage as: "Therefore, just as through one person sin came into the world, and through sin death. And so death passed on to all people, *in that all sinned.*" He interpreted the *in quo* in the last phrase in a conditional sense: Adam's descendants die if they follow his example and sin as he did.[2]

Augustine provided summaries of Pelagius's positions: Every human is said to be endowed with the power or ability to will and to do the good. "Our ability to say and think what is good comes from God, who gave us this power, and also assists it.[3] God endowed humans with a free will that is so strong and resolute that it can resist sin—without denying our enduring need of God's help.[4] "Man can be without sin, and can keep the commandments of God, if he so wills wishes, since God has given that ability."[5] Pelagius maintains that humans can be sinless by their own effort and the grace of God: for him, grace means the state or condition in which humans were created by God with free will.[6] There is "no inherited evil in us, and we are born without fault."[7]

Augustine's reading of Romans 5:12 led him to a very different conclusion: "The Apostle declares, 'Sin entered into the world through one man, and through sin came death, and so it passed on to all men, for in him all sinned.'...since all were already united with him by that power to procreate them with which he was endowed."[8] Augustine asserted that when Adam sinned, the whole human race was in his loins. In accord with the laws of heredity, "those who were in his loins [in his sperm] and were to come into this world through the concupiscence [sexual urge] of the flesh were condemned with him."[9] Augustine declared that, since every human is conceived through concupiscence, the offspring of even a baptized parent is born carnal. All future humans are born with the effects of Adam's sin, "since a man begets physically through the lustful passion [libido] of his body."[10] In Augustine's thinking, the guilt of concupiscence had been removed from the baptized parents, but the guilt coming from Adam's sin remains in the infant until it is forgiven in baptism.[11] The sin of the first man perverted our nature; it not only became sinful but also generates sinners. The effect of the first sin is thus comparable to a genetic disease that parents transmit by inheritance.[12] Augustine proclaimed that "no one is set free from the mass of perdition, which results from the first Adam, unless he has the gift which he can only receive by the grace of the Savior."[13] "Freewill is capable of evil, but incapable of good, unless it is assisted by the all-powerful good."[14]

Augustine maintained that the grievousness of Adam's fall was in proportion to the loftiness of his position. His nature was to be capable of immortality if he had refused to sin. There was no conflict of flesh against spirit nor any struggle against vice because there was no vice in him. His sin was much worse than the sins of all other humans simply because he was so much better than all others.[15] He had the ability not to sin, not to die, not to forsake the good. His sin was a fall from a lofty perfection.[16]

Earlier, in the latter part of the second century, Irenaeus of Lyon wrote five books *Against Heresies* (*Adversus Haereses*), refuting the teachings of Gnosticism. Gnostics maintained that an inferior deity had created the material world, which they considered to be a radically evil realm of darkness. They offered initiates a secret knowledge (*gnosis*) or enlightenment that would enable their inner spark of heavenly light to escape its imprisonment in the body and to ascend to union with the transcendent, true God in a spiritual realm of light.

In his refutation, Irenaeus stressed the goodness of material creation and particularly of our bodies united with a soul filled with God's Spirit. He attributed the goodness of matter and our bodies to God the Father, who bestows existence on all things by his own decision and free act.[17] Irenaeus offered an instructive analogy. Just as water is needed to unite dry flour into a piece of dough, or a loaf, we who are many cannot be made one in Christ

Jesus without the water that comes from heaven. In baptism, our bodies receive the unity that brings immortality by means of the washing; our souls receive it by the reception of God's Spirit. Both are needed, for it is the material body united with the soul imbued with God's Spirit that together advance humans' progress toward the life of God (*AH* 3,17,2).

Irenaeus emphasized that humans are not spiritual by the abolition of the flesh. A complete human, made in the image and likeness of God, comprises a soul or spirit permeated by God's outpoured Spirit united with a created material body (*AH* 5,6,1). Irenaeus saw the communion and unity of flesh and spirit as analogous to the Eucharist. The bread, which comes from the earth, receives the invocation (*epiclēsis*) of God's Spirit, and then it is no longer common bread but Eucharist, consisting of two things, earthly and heavenly (*AH* 4,18,5).

Irenaeus especially emphasized that God made humans free from the beginning. Made in the likeness of God, who is free, they have their own power of choice. God upholds their free and unconstrained choice in their actions and even in their coming to faith. Humans freely choose to do the good that God intends, without compulsion from God (*AH* 4.37.1). God is good, merciful, and *patient* (*AH* 3,25,3).

In contrast to Augustine's understanding of Adam's sin as a fall from a lofty perfection, Irenaeus considered newly created humans to have been infantile and immature, and not yet prepared for an adult way of life. God had the power to impart perfection at the beginning, but man, being like a child, was incapable of receiving it or retaining it (*AH* 4, 38,1 & 2). He had to grow into full maturity (*Apostolic Preaching* 12). Humans learned the distinction between good and evil by experience, so that they might make their own decision to choose the better path (*AH* 4,39,1). God's love is what leads us to God (*AH* 4,20,1).

Irenaeus's perspectives on human freedom and development are remarkably compatible with the contemporary understanding of the evolutionary development of humans. His perspectives can likewise be integrated with Augustine's core insight that there is an inherent, problematic ambiguity in humans' exercise of freedom. Pelagius emphasized that humans had the ability to do good; all they had to do was will it and they would be good. Augustine rightly pointed to the dark side of humans' exercise of freedom. He stressed the degree of sinfulness in the world. Evil seems to be universal and irradicable in history. However, Augustine's descriptive construct, that all future humans were in Adam's loins and that we inherit the guilt of Adam's sin because we are all born through sexual intercourse, is no longer tenable.

Augustine constructed his theology of original sin on an inaccurate Latin translation of the original Greek text of Romans 5:12. The last phrase in Greek, ἐφ' ᾧ πάντες ἥμαρτον ("inasmuch as all sinned") was rendered as *in quo omnes peccaverunt*, which Augustine interpreted to mean "in him all sinned." Locating all future humans in Adam's sperm, Augustine concluded that all humans inherit the guilt of Adam's "original sin" by the fact that they are conceived through sexual intercourse. That line of thinking, focused on sperm and sexual libido, is no longer supported by Romans 5:12. In 1979, the Vatican issued the *Nova Vulgata* translation that replaced *in quo omnes peccaverunt* (in him all sinned) with *eo quod omnes peccaverunt* (because or inasmuch as all sinned).[18] There is need for new thinking.

A CODETERMINED FREEDOM

In *Foundations of Christian Faith*, Karl Rahner located his treatment of "original sin" within the framework of human freedom and responsibility. Our freedom is not actualized in isolation from the world of persons. "It is co-determined by the free history of all the others who constitute [our] own unique world of persons….Consequently, the guilt of others is a permanent factor in the situation and realm of the individual's freedom, for the latter are

determined by [our] personal world." Since the origins of humanity, freedom has been influenced by the guilt arising from the decisions of those who preceded us or were around us: "[The] shared
situation of freedom can become an intrinsic moment in the free
decision of another."[19] Unfounded, negative judgments about persons outside one's own group affect the thinking, decisions, and
actions of others. That is the origin of prejudice, persecution, and
worse. They all involve sharing in a situation codetermined by
guilt laden choices. "The situation of our own freedom bears the
stamp of the guilt of others in a way which cannot be eradicated."[20]
In the concrete history of the human race, there is "no real possibility of ever overcoming once and for all this determination of the
situation of freedom by guilt."[21] "Original sin, therefore, expresses
nothing else but the historical origin of the present, universal and
ineradicable situation of our freedom as co-determined by guilt."
Because this situation has a history universally determined by
guilt, "God's self-communication in grace comes to [humans] not
from 'Adam,' not from the beginning of the human race, but from
the goal of this history, from the God-Man Jesus Christ."[22]

Gabriel Daly speaks of a sinful history in which new generations add their own contributions to the historical pool of hatred
and persecution:

> Often they do so in the name of distorted values con-
> ceived of diseased imaginations. Such values may even
> parody the values of religion and use its symbols. One
> has only to think of the Nazi swastika or the fiery cross
> of the Ku Klux Klan. The manic response of people at the
> Nuremberg rallies and the ludicrous prancing of small-
> town businessmen wearing white sheets witness not
> only to prejudice but also to the daimonic, pre-rational,
> and unhealed psychic forces which seek release in ritu-
> alised hatred, fear, and scapegoating. Children living in
> communities which ritualise their phobias and aggres-

sive instincts will naturally and unconsciously take the diseased moral environment for normal.[23]

Disowning such a diseased environment and seeking reconciliation with the scapegoats, will bring God's forgiveness and redemption.

THEOLOGICAL EXPOSITION: HUMAN EVOLUTIONARY HISTORY

Denis Edwards has formulated a theological exposition of "original sin" linked to the perspectives of evolutionary science regarding the emergence of humans.[24] He relates our cultural and genetic inheritance to René Girard's analysis of violence in terms of the "scapegoat mechanism," in which a community unites against a common enemy.[25] He proceeds by turning to the biologist Ernst Mayr, who has described the evolution of humans in relation to the increase in brain size. "In Neanderthals, who were taller and more robust, brain size reached 1,600 cc, but the relative brain size was a little less than that of *H. sapiens*."[26] Enhancement of intelligence and communication provided a survival advantage. And the need for extended parental care of infants born with undeveloped brains served to pass on nongenetic information. "Learning and the transfer of cultural information became an intrinsic dimension of human life."[27]

Edwards also turns to the perspectives of Edward O. Wilson, a biologist who studies the genetic foundation of the social behavior of animals and humans.[28] Wilson speaks of "'epigenetic rules' which are hereditary regularities in our brains that bias our cultural evolution in certain ways." Our cultural life is shaped in part by genetic dispositions, but culture also shapes the genetic inheritance of the human community. "Culture helps to select the mutating and recombining genes that underlie human nature."[29] In other words, culture is a large part of what shapes human evolution.

In humans, some genetic tendencies, such as territorial expansion and defense, are so powerful that they give rise to cultural universals in human societies. War at the level of tribes and cities (think Florence and Sienna) is rarer now. But territory is often the issue in conflicts between countries. Wilson notes, "War arises from both genes and culture and can best be avoided by a thorough understanding of the manner in which these two modes of heredity interact within different historical contexts."[30]

In primates, intelligence is related to social interaction. Changes in brain size, language skills, social organization and means of subsistence were all interrelated. Those who had a sharper consciousness would have had greater social and reproductive success. The ability to read others and empathy, an awareness of how others feel, were valuable for survival. One could judge who was friend or foe.[31]

Brain development and language gave small groups of early humans the ability to cooperate and mutually support and defend one another. There was care for children, and altruism for kin and for members of one's close-knit social group. A tendency toward mutual support and cooperation had been selected as an advantage in human evolutionary history. But natural selection did not favor love, compassion, or help to outsiders. The genetic tendency from our evolutionary past involves benevolent behavior toward insiders and hostility toward outsiders as competitors or enemies. As Raymund Schwager observes, the exclusion of others and a tendency to violence has become part of our cultural and genetic inheritance. In the course of our evolutionary history, "sin has become woven into the natural tendencies of human life."[32] Consider the historical violence and repression that many white persons inflicted on Black persons during the Reconstruction after the Civil War, and still do, even today.

Mayr proposes the need for a *transformation* of our evolutionary inheritance. He insists that the outcry of a prophet or the teaching of a philosopher is required to move humans to include outsiders in their concern and commitment.[33] There is need for an enlightenment that casts away polarizing attitudes and biases instilled over generations.

RETHINKING AUGUSTINE'S ASSUMPTIONS

Augustine had declared that without the gift of grace by baptism, one could not be saved. In his view, most humans, whom he called "a mass of perdition," were bound for damnation. In Augustine's theological construct, baptism released one from a state in which a relationship with God was impossible. That included those "who have not heard the Gospel" and infants who died before being baptized.[34] In his letter to Jerome, Augustine noted that thousands of souls leave the bodies of dying children who are unbaptized and asked whether it is fair that such unbaptized infants should be condemned, since they had not committed any personal sin.[35] Augustine might have asked whether God would implement the colossal number of condemnations that he was postulating. Jesus came not to call the virtuous but sinners (Mark 2:17).

In 2007, the International Theological Commission noted that the medieval conception of limbo for unbaptized infants had moderated Augustine's position but upheld an unduly restricted view of salvation. The document, entitled "The Hope for Salvation for Infants Who Die without Being Baptized," instead proposed "strong grounds for hope that God will save infants when we have not been able to do for them what we would have wished to do, namely, to baptize them into the faith and life of the Church."[36] Creation has always been graced because it is the expression of God's self-giving love.[37] God's Spirit has invited *all* humans to a relationship of love from the time of their origin. It is unthinkable that such a God would not embrace unbaptized infants who have died.

Contemporary theology emphasizes that God created so that *others* might have the freedom to love, and to live in relationships. Humans can love because God has loved them. But, as Irenaeus noted, early humans were like infants who had to grow and learn through experience. They had to expand the horizon of their trust and their relationships to include *others* outside their kin, clan, or tribe. They had to learn to welcome strangers, instead of scapegoating them as threats or enemies. The human potential for empathy and caring was always grounded in a transcendental openness to God, which initially was not reflectively recognized or conceptually articulated. Openness to the God who is freedom and love was expressed in humans love and care for one another before they developed any explicit concept of God or realized that they were invited to respond to God's love. The earliest human encounter with the personal reality we call God was likely actualized implicitly and pre-reflectively in prehistoric gestures of openness to the needs of another human, especially a stranger. The way humans treat one another has always been indicative of their opening or closing of self to a relationship with God (1 John 4:20).[38]

REFUSING TO LOVE OTHERS THE WAY GOD LOVES US

In Luke's version of the debate about which is the first or greatest commandment, a lawyer asks Jesus, "Teacher, what must I do to inherit eternal life?" Jesus asks the lawyer how he reads what is written in the law. The lawyer answers, "You shall love the Lord your God" with all your heart, soul, strength, and mind, "and your neighbor as yourself." Jesus replies that he has answered correctly. But the lawyer asks, "Who is my neighbor?" Jesus responds with a parable in which a Samaritan, and not a priest or Levite, stopped and cared for the stranger who had been assaulted (Luke 10:30–37). Jesus then asks, who was the neighbor that showed love? The neighbor in the parable was a scapegoated outsider, whom many Jews of the time despised and considered ritually impure.

Scapegoating of outsiders is an ingrained human tendency. Some have embraced the notion of white supremacy. In *Gaudium et*

Spes, the Second Vatican Council declared that humanity's growing mastery over nature, as well as its shaping of the world's political, social, and economic order, is overshadowed by injustice, unfair distribution, and widespread hunger. Noble deeds are matched by villainous, progress contends with decline, and brotherhood and sisterhood coexist with hatred (sections 4 and 9). Total emancipation is clearly not to be expected through human effort alone, and a purely earthly paradise will not be established, since every individual human, and thus all humans together, bring a divided self to the struggle with good and evil, having a freedom weakened by sin. Nevertheless, humans have the freedom to turn themselves toward what is good (sections 10, 13, and 17).

In Jesus, God offered anew and in an unsurpassable way the self-giving relationship initiated in the act of creating. In the fullness of his humanity, Jesus was the definitive revelation and self-communication of God (Col 1:15). What he did—eating and drinking with sinners and outcasts—and said—"Love your neighbor as yourself" (Mark 12:31)—actualized the divine plan of love and mercy (Eph 1:3–11). Jesus declared that it was not the healthy or righteous who needed his healing but the sick or sinners (Mark 2:17). In him, God's initiative of self-revelation, inviting us to be friends both with God and with one another (Exod 33:11; John 15:14–15), achieved its fullness.[39] In his human freedom, Jesus irrevocably responded to God's gift of love and actualized the possibilities it offered to all humans. That was achieved with self-emptying effort amid the events of his life. The Epistle to the Hebrews tells of Jesus truly sharing in the human condition, through temptation, suffering, and death (Heb 4:15—5:9). Through his crucifixion he became the innocent victim who forgives.

The risen Christ draws us to the side of victims and the excluded! As the beaten and battered but forgiving victim, Jesus invites and challenges us to embrace a new way of life of mutual forgiveness that puts an end to scapegoating. To be human is to need forgiveness. Jesus offers the saving healing of "*undergoing* being forgiven" so that we, in turn, can forgive.[40] We are formed into an *inclusive* community filled with God's Spirit, witnessing to a new creation and to divine nonviolent love. Edwards thus concludes, "As a tendency to sin is built into communal life by way of our cultural and genetic inheritance, so nonviolent liberating love is to be lived out in the community of those born again of the Spirit" (John 3:1–10).[41] The washing of baptism is more like amniotic fluid *for* rebirth in the Spirit and the illumination emphasized by Justin Martyr than a washing away.

Original sin did not just happen in a garden at the beginning of human existence. It is the foundational sin that happens every day in the world. It is the ever-present virus in the human exercise of freedom, manifested in spurious claims of superiority or supremacy over and hatred of "others." It is at the core of racism, scapegoating, victimization, and wars over territory. It is the foundational refusal to love others.

In Jesus, God became a human who was beaten, battered, mocked, and crucified, but still reaffirmed his love for the God he called Abba, and for all humans, even as he hung on the cross. He lived in a way that had always been possible for all humans. His way of living and dying proclaimed that when we give of ourselves for one another, we are imaging God's love for us. Openness to the God who is the source of freedom and love empowers our freedom to live that divine way of being human. We can choose to see one another in the way that God sees us. We can choose to act like the Samaritan (or in our culture, a Black or homosexual person) who stops to help a stranger seen as a neighbor.

5

FREEDOM ANNULLED BY HUMAN SOCIETY

Slavery and the Repression of Women

GOD CREATED FREEDOM and possibility; humans invented slavery and repression. John Noonan has documented how, for centuries, the Church resisted condemning slavery.[1] Tracing the acceptance and practice of slavery in the Catholic tradition, Noonan begins by juxtaposing a consideration of slavery as once "an unknown sin" within the Church with the fact that it is presently "regarded with horror as the blackest kind of affront to the human person and among the most serious derelictions of duty to God, whose image is the person."[2] Noonan starts from an analysis of the Hebrew Scriptures, and then proceeds through a consideration of the Gospels, the epistles of Paul, the early Church, medieval theologians and canonists, and the European slave trade, particularly in the time of colonial expansion. He documents how popes received slaves, offered them as gifts, and used them to man "the galleys of the pope's navy"—observing that slavery existed in the Papal States into the early nineteenth century.[3] Missionaries and their religious orders, traveling in the path of Portuguese and Spanish explorers, engaged in the buying and selling of slaves, and even complained at attempts to limit the number of slaves they could own. The ownership and selling of slaves was likewise practiced by the Jesuits and others in the United States.[4]

Glimmers of opposition emerged. Immanuel Kant condemned slavery and the hypocrisy of the nations that controlled the sugar islands. He declared that persons were never to be used as if they were mere tools or things. They had "inborn rights which are inalienable and belong necessarily to humanity."[5] A case against slavery emerged outside the Catholic Church in 1693, at the monthly meeting of Friends in Philadelphia. Quakers took up the cause of abolition and emancipation.[6] Then, in the culture of late eighteenth-century England, Jesus's commandment of love finally began to make significant inroads against the institution of slavery.

As Noonan notes, there were ten distinct condemnations of usury—charging interest for loans—in the Catholic tradition (which, with the rise of capitalism, came to be accepted) but no clear and definitive condemnation of slavery. Pope Gregory XVI's prohibition of the slave trade, in his letter *In Supremo Apostolatus Fastigio*, was issued in 1839 at the behest of the British government.[7] The papal letter only focused on the slave trade. In the mindset of the time, slavery was not considered intrinsically evil within the Catholic tradition, since Paul sent Philemon's slave, Onesimus, back to him (Phlm 10–18). John England, bishop of Charleston, whose diocese also included Georgia and North Carolina, emphasized that the pope had in mind the international trade; the southern states "have not engaged in the negro traffic." England insisted that the Catholic Church had always accepted domestic slavery; it was not "incompatible with the natural law"; and, when title to a slave was justly acquired, it was lawful "in the eye of heaven."[8] That was not the position of Daniel O'Connell, who advocated freedom for Ireland and equally freedom for Blacks![9] But, as recently as 1936 and 1960, Catholic moral theologians were still arguing that slavery was "less fitting" for human dignity but "not per se opposed to natural law," and "not unlawful by Scripture."[10]

For centuries, the Catholic Church accepted, participated in, and even defended the cultural institution of slavery. The Second Vatican Council finally referred to slavery as evil in the Constitution on the Church in the Modern World, *Gaudium et Spes* (section 27). And Pope John Paul II condemned slavery as intrinsically evil in *Veritatis Splendor* (section 80), Noonan observes that "the magisterium came into harmony with the thinking of the body of the faithful." Average Catholics thought and still think that the Church had always been against slavery. In reality, rank and file believers' perspectives on that issue were ahead of the official thinking. "By 1960, everyone knew that slavery was bad."[11]

The Second Vatican Council's positive appraisal of human autonomy in *Gaudium et Spes* (sections 36, 41, 56) represented a breakthrough regarding the modern history of freedom. The Declaration on Religious Freedom, *Dignitatis Humanae* (sections 2, 9–10), further recognized the autonomy of the human and the rights of the person over against the previous emphasis on the rights of truth.

The autonomy or freedom of humans comes from their creation by God in God's image (Gen 1:26). As discussed in previous chapters, the randomness and chance in the evolutionary process enables human freedom, including the freedom to believe. And as Walter Kasper observes, for Paul, "Jesus Christ is the likeness of God that brings to fulfilment the human likeness to God given with creation" (2 Cor 4.4; Col 1:15; Heb 1:3). Kasper concludes, "According to this biblical viewpoint, then, the dignity of human beings lies in their freedom."[12]

But, as Kasper observes, "Like all great ideas, the idea of the autonomy [freedom] grounded in creation needed time before it could become a part of general opinion."[13] In the era before the Second Vatican Council, "the liberating impulses of the gospel remained ineffective in wide areas of life. Slavery and serfdom, as well as the inferior view of women, continued to be legitimated for many centuries. Religious freedom and liberty of conscience were denied to Jews and heretics."[14]

"The starting point and the stimulant of modern thinking is freedom…freedom is not merely a human characteristic or capacity. It is a transcendental definition of the human being…it is the condition of being human *per se*."[15] And only when we think of freedom as liberation have we arrived at the Christian understanding of what freedom is: "For freedom Christ has set us free" (Gal 5:1; John 8:36).[16]

MYTHS UPHOLDING THE REPRESSION OF WOMEN: SEDUCTIVE SOURCE OF EVIL

There has been a longstanding patriarchal culture persistently undermining the freedom and dignity of women. It was sustained, within Judaism and then in Christianity, by narratives that disparaged, vilified, and scapegoated women.[17] The third chapter of the Book of Genesis tells the story of a serpent who engages a woman in conversation and induces her to eat the fruit of the only forbidden tree in the garden, the tree of the knowledge of good and evil.[18] The woman also gives some to her husband.

In Genesis, Adam and Eve become ashamed of their nakedness and fail in their attempt to hide from God (Gen 3:7, 10–11). God confronts the woman and asks her what she has done. She replies, "The serpent tricked me, and I ate" (Gen 3:13). After cursing the serpent, God turns to the woman: "I will greatly increase your pangs in childbearing; in pain you shall bring forth children, yet your desire shall be for your husband, and he shall rule over you" (Gen 3:16).

Male authors in a patriarchal society explained the de facto existence of evil by indicting woman as its source and thereby developed a justification for maintaining the cultural facts of male dominance and female subservience. Stories about Eve's primeval duping of Adam buttressed male hegemony because Eve's supposed role in causing Adam's downfall became a tool for domination. Every woman became an Eve, indicted as the cause of evil and the corrupter of men and even angels.

In the second century before the Christian era, Jewish interest in the cause of evil was heightened. Rabbinic literature and apocalyptic works developed imaginative "retellings" of Genesis. The pseudonymous *1 Enoch* or *Ethiopic Apocalypse of Enoch* (dated second century BCE–first century CE) contains only passing references to the Garden of Eden narrative.[19] It instead uses Genesis 6:1–4 as the starting point for explaining the origins of evil:

> When people began to multiply on the face of the ground, and daughters were born to them, the sons of God saw that they were fair; and they took wives for themselves of all that they chose. Then the Lord said, "My spirit shall not abide in mortals forever, for they are flesh; their days shall be one hundred twenty years." The Nephilim were on the earth in those days—and also afterward—when the sons of God went in to the daughters of humans, who bore children to them. These were the heroes that were of old, warriors of renown.

1 Enoch presents an embellished version of the Nephilim myth in chapters 6—11, 15, and 106:14–18.[20] The "sons of God" are angels, or immortal, spiritual watchers, who descended from heaven to satisfy their lust for the beautiful women of earth. Having entered a mutual pact to carry out rape with their leader Semyaz, two hundred watchers descended upon Mount Hermon. They slept with the women of earth, defiled themselves, and revealed all kinds of charms and enchantments to the women (*1 Enoch* 6:6—7:2; 16:2–3). The women gave birth to giants, three thousand ells tall, who turned against humankind and filled the earth with blood and lawlessness (7:2–6). One of the fallen watchers, Azazel, who in certain passages is called "leader," taught men to make "swords and knives, and shields, and breastplates." He taught women about "bracelets, decorations, (shadowing of the eye) with antimony, ornamentation, the beautifying of the eyelids, all kinds of precious stones, and all coloring tinctures" (8:1; 10:7–8).[21] War, jewelry, cosmetics, and sex were Azazel's lessons. And, as in Genesis and the *Odyssey*, evil, women, and knowledge are presented as a package deal.

The *Book of Jubilees* (second century BCE), an embellished commentary, interpreting and paraphrasing Genesis, retains *1 Enoch*'s account of the origin of evil but with some modifications.[22] In *Jubilees*, God himself sent the angels, or watchers, "to teach the sons of man, and perform judgment and uprightness upon the earth" (*Jub.* 4:15; 5:6). Only later did they choose wives from the daughters of men, who bore them sons that were giants (5:1; 4:22). "And injustice increased upon the earth, and all flesh corrupted its way, men and cattle and beasts and birds…and every imagination of the thoughts of all mankind was thus continually evil" (5:2).[23] To remedy the situation, the fallen angels were bound in the depths of the earth (5:6). All humans except Noah and those in the ark were destroyed by a flood, while the giants slew each other by the sword of war that God sent into their midst (5:6–9).

As in *1 Enoch*, the spirits of those sons of the disobedient watchers lived on and began to lead the children of Noah's sons into error (7:27; 10:1–2).[24] After Noah's intercession on behalf of his sons, God casts nine-tenths of the evil spirits, or demons, who are "cruel and were created to destroy," into the place of judgment. He makes an agreement with their chief, Mastema, or Satan, permitting 10 percent of them to remain on earth to assist him in corrupting and leading astray the wicked until the time of his final judgment (10:3–9). Only in the time of the messianic kingdom will men finally live in peace and joy, "and there will be no Satan and no evil (one) who will destroy" (23:29).

Chapter 3 of *Jubilees*, which some consider its primitive core, also contains the fall story of Adam and Eve with only minor differences from the narrative in Genesis 3.[25] The Garden of Eden story of Genesis 3 relates the first instance of evil in the world and is kept separate from the watcher myth of Genesis 6.[26] In this stage of development, the serpent and Satan remain distinct figures in two different stories. The focus on women will now be pushed to new heights, or I should say "new lows."

The Testament of Reuben, from the *Testaments of the Twelve Patriarchs* (second century BCE), claims to convey the directives that Reuben gave to his sons on his deathbed.[27] He instructs them not to devote their attention to a woman's looks, not to live with a woman who is already married, and not to become involved in affairs with women (3:10) nor attend to their beauty (4:1). He offers the following reflections:

> For women are evil, my children, and by reason of their lacking authority or power over man, they scheme treacherously how they might entice him to themselves by means of their looks. And whomever they cannot enchant by their appearance they conquer by a stratagem. Indeed, the angel of the Lord told me and instructed me that women are more easily overcome by the spirit of promiscuity than are men. They contrive in their hearts against men, then by decking themselves out they lead men's minds astray, by a look they implant their poison, and finally in the act itself they take them captive. For a woman is not able to coerce a man overtly, but by a harlot's manner she accomplishes her villainy. Accordingly, my children, flee from sexual promiscuity, and order your wives and your daughters not to adorn their heads and their appearances so as to deceive men's sound minds. For every woman who schemes in these ways is destined for eternal punishment. For it was thus that they charmed the Watchers, who were before the flood. As they continued looking at the women, they were filled with desire for them and perpetrated the act in their minds. Then they were transformed into human males, and while the women were cohabiting with their husbands they appeared to

them. Since the women's minds were filled with lust for these apparitions, they gave birth to giants. For the Watchers were disclosed to them as being as high as the heavens. (5:1–6)

These perspectives are offered by a man who has just confessed that he once watched his father Jacob's concubine, Bilhah, bathing in a secluded place and became obsessed by her naked femininity. Later, when Jacob went to visit his father, Isaac, and Bilhah had become intoxicated and was sound asleep, naked in her bed, Reuben went in and raped her, without her being aware of it. He left her sleeping soundly (3:11–14; cf. Gen 35:22). Given such a disclosure, it is astounding that Reuben could declare, "Women are more easily overcome by promiscuity than are men"! The sequence in the narrative reflects the appalling mindset of the male author.

The watcher legend has been revised in this text. Women are now declared to be instigators of the watchers' fall and to be directly responsible for the subsequent spread of evil because of their seductive wiles. In *1 Enoch*, Azazel, the fallen angel, taught the use of cosmetics and beauty aids after the molestation. In the Testament of Reuben, women use them to seduce the angels.[28]

Explaining the source of evil by embellishing the myth of the giants in Genesis 6 gradually faded away. Jewish apocalyptic literature and rabbinic literature used a variety of models for explaining evil in the world. In subsequent works, the fall story of Adam and Eve, from Genesis 3, again predominated, but elements from the watcher myth were retained and integrated into the interpretation of Genesis 3. In Eve's description of the fall in the *Apocalypse of Moses* (first century CE), the serpent is presented as a vessel of Satan.[29] Satan induces the serpent to become his vessel so that he can speak words through the serpent's mouth to deceive Adam (*Apoc. Moses* 16–17). But his only way of getting to Adam, whom he envies, is through Eve, when she is alone in her female section of paradise. Speaking through the serpent, Satan convinces her that by eating the fruit of the one forbidden tree she will be like God and know good and evil. Once Eve is anxious to eat the fruit, he changes his mind. Only if she swears an oath that she will give the fruit to Adam will he let her have it (*Apoc. Moses* 15; 17:1— 19:2).[30] Eve agrees and says, "When he had received the oath from me, he went, climbed the tree, and sprinkled his evil poison on the fruit which he gave me to eat which is his covetousness" (19:3). Eve immediately experiences shame at her nakedness and covers herself with fig leaves (20:5). But she still shares her secret with Adam and persuades him also to eat the fruit (21:1–5). Adam eats and his eyes are opened. He realizes his nakedness, and says, "O evil woman! Why have you wrought destruction among us? You have estranged me from the glory of God" (21:6).

The plea for mercy that God prescribes for Eve when he confronts her is significant: "Lord, Lord, save me, and I will never again turn to the sin of the flesh." God then responds, "And by this, according to your word I will judge you, because of the enmity which the enemy has placed in you" (25:3–4). The serpent then loses his hands and feet (26). Eve's prescribed confession suggests that Satan sexually seduced her. So does a remark made by Adam in the related Latin *Life of Adam and Eve*: "Eve's complaint has come to me; perhaps again the serpent has contended with her" (20:1). The sexual element of the watcher legend has been blended into the Adam and Eve story, and the serpent is now identified as Satan, a fallen angel.

In sections 12 to 17 of the Latin *Life of Adam and Eve*, Satan explains why he deceived Eve and, with her assistance, caused Adam to be expelled from the garden of Paradise. Satan had refused to worship Adam as the image and likeness of God. Even Michael's urgings had not been able to convince him to worship what he considered inferior and younger in creation. Having been cast out of heaven, Satan was determined to rise above God by corrupting man, God's created image, whom he now envied. Both the *Apocalypse of Moses* and the Latin *Life of Adam and Eve* idealize

Adam. Eve is constantly lamenting that she has brought misfortune, sickness, and death to Adam by her misdeed.[31] Adam doesn't let her forget it, and even orders her to tell their children how she caused the fall (*Apoc. Moses* 14:2–3; see also 7:1–3). In the *Life of Adam and Eve*, Eve asks Adam if he would like to kill her for what she did. Adam replies, "Rather let us rise and search for ourselves, how we might live, and not weaken" (3:2–3). The woman continues to be presented as responsible for evil, connected in some way with the theme of female seduction.

The *Slavonic Apocalypse of Enoch* (*2 Enoch* or *Book of the Secrets of Enoch*—ca. late first century CE) consists of a series of visions in which apostate angels and their leader, Satanail, play a prominent role.[32] As in the *Apocalypse of Moses*, elements from the watcher legend are again interwoven with the fall of Adam (*2 Enoch* 7, 18, 29). We are told that Satan first tried to set his throne above God's, for which he and his heavenly cohorts were banished to the underworld. This took place before the angels sinned with the daughters of men, for which Satan is also held responsible. That deed, now secondary and subsequent to the fall of Adam and Eve, was the climax of Satanail's campaign to corrupt the earth. He had already brought evil to earth, motivated by his envy of Adam's lordship over that part of creation: "And he [Satanail] became aware of his condemnation and the sin which he sinned previously. And that is why he thought up the scheme against Adam. In such a form he entered paradise and corrupted [seduced?] Eve. But Adam he did not contact" (*2 Enoch* 31:6). Eve brought death to Adam (*2 Enoch* 30:17).

In the *Apocalypse of Abraham* (14, 23–24), the fall of Adam and Eve is the starting point for the history of the human race.[33] We again meet Azazel acting as the teacher of secrets, the role he was assigned in *1 Enoch*. The fall, which he instigates by revealing his secrets, seems identified with sexual union between Adam and Eve. This same motif seems reflected in *2 Baruch* or *Syriac Apocalypse of Baruch* (early second century CE), which states that the conception of children and the sexual passion of parents are results of the transgression of Adam (*2 Bar.* 56:6).[34]

Except for the third and sixth chapters of Genesis, all the sources cited above, dated from the second century BCE to the second century CE, were apocryphal or pseudepigraphal (falsely attributed to a past figure, such as Enoch). There was almost no development of themes from Genesis in the canonical Hebrew Scriptures. Only the contemporaneous books of Ecclesiasticus or Wisdom of Jesus Ben Sirach and the Wisdom of Solomon, accepted as canonical by Catholic Christians, contain pertinent references. Ecclesiasticus, or the Wisdom of Jesus Ben Sirach (translated into Greek after 132 BCE) declares, "From a woman sin had its beginning, and because of her we all die" (25:24–26). In the next breath, the author speaks of male domination and female subservience: "Allow no outlet to water, and no boldness of speech to an evil wife. If she does not go as you direct, separate her from yourself."[35] The Wisdom of Solomon (first century BCE) says that death entered the world through the envy of the devil (see Wis 2:23–24).

JESUS VALUED WOMEN AND WOMEN VALUED HIM

Jesus is remembered as being unreservedly positive in his attitude toward and relationship with women. He healed Peter's mother-in-law (Mark 1:30–31). He likened his meals with tax collectors and sinners to a woman who searched for a lost silver coin and then celebrated with her friends and neighbors (Luke 15:8–10). He definitively rejected Rabbi Hillel's teaching that a man could divorce his wife for any cause, no matter how trivial (Matt 19:3–9). He is presented interacting with a Syrophoenician (Canaanite) woman, who stood her ground and got what she asked for: Jesus healed her daughter (Mark 7:24–30; Matt 15:21–28). A woman who suffered from a hemorrhage for twelve years touched his garments and was healed. Jesus told her to go in peace (Mark 5:25–34; Matt 9:20–22; Luke 8:43–48).

Jesus is called the Christ (Messiah or Anointed). It was an anonymous woman that poured nard, a costly ointment, on his head at Bethany in the house of Simon the leper (Mark 14:3–9; Matt 26:6–13). In the Gospel of John 12:1–8, Mary, the sister of Lazarus, is said to have anointed Jesus's feet (John 12:1–8). In Luke 7:36–50, it was an anonymous "woman in the city," who was a sinner, that anointed his feet. Conflating the name Mary with "the woman in the city," Gregory the Great erroneously identified the woman as Mary Magdalene, whom he thereby wrongly branded as a prostitute.

Women were among Jesus's friends and followers. He had a close relationship with Martha and Mary, the sisters of Lazarus (John 11:1–44). In Luke 10:38–42, we read,

> He entered a certain village, where a woman named Martha welcomed him into her home. She had a sister named Mary, who sat at the Lord's feet and listened to what he was saying. But Martha was distracted by her many tasks; so she came to him and asked, "Lord, do you not care that my sister has left me to do all the work by myself? Tell her then to help me." But the Lord answered her, "Martha, Martha, you are worried and distracted by many things; there is need of only one thing. Mary has chosen the better part, which will not be taken away from her."

The scene presents Mary intellectually engaged with Jesus's teaching, and Jesus championed her engagement. He did not subscribe to the stereotypes embraced by the foremost intellectual of that time, Philo of Alexandria, who characterized masculine thoughts as "wise, sound, just, prudent, pious, filled with freedom and boldness, and kin to wisdom…the female sex is irrational and akin to bestial passions, fear, sorrow, pleasure and desire, from which ensue incurable weaknesses and indescribable diseases."[36]

In Luke 8:1–3, we read that the Twelve *and a group of women* accompanied Jesus as he moved through cities and villages: "Mary, called Magdalene, from whom seven demons had gone out [epileptic seizures?], and Joanna, the wife of Herod's steward Chuza, and Susanna, and many others, who provided for them out of their resources."

Mark and Matthew report that women who had followed Jesus in and from Galilee, ministering to him, were "looking on from a distance" as Jesus hung on the cross. Only three are named: Mary Magdalene, Mary the mother of James and Joseph, and Salome (Mark 15:40), whom Matthew refers to as the mother of the sons of Zebedee (Matt 27:56). John 19:25 lists four women: Jesus's mother, his mother's sister (Salome, the wife of Zebedee and mother of James and John), Mary the wife of Clopas, and Mary Magdalene.[37] In the second century, Hegesippus attested that Clopas was the brother of Joseph, the husband of Jesus's mother.[38] In other words, Jesus's mother, an aunt who was his mother's sister, an aunt who was Joseph's sister-in-law, and Mary Magdalene were possibly there. Their presence during that tragic event showed how much those women cared for Jesus.

Mary Magdalene and Mary the mother of [James and] Joses saw the tomb where Jesus's body was laid (Mark 15:47; Matt 27:61). That tomb was empty when they returned, along with Salome and Joanna, early on Sunday morning (Matt 28:1; Mark 16:1; Luke 24:10). John names only Mary Magdalene, but she uses the pronoun *we* (John 20:1–2). Matthew and John then report that the first appearance of the risen Jesus was to the women near the tomb (Matt 28:9–10; John 20:4–18). In Paul's earlier account in 1 Corinthians 15:5–8, Jesus is said to have first appeared to Peter, but no women are mentioned in Paul's list. In the mindset of the time, women's testimony as witnesses was not credible. The fact that two Gospels present women as witnesses of Jesus's resurrection likely points to a historical memory: fabricating such testimony would have been counterproductive at that time.

Jesus's relationship with women ignited an awakening. In the decades after Jesus's death and resurrection, Paul introduced Phoebe as deacon of the church at Cenchreae and referred to Junia as prominent among the apostles (Rom 16:1, 7). Women of means, such as Mary, mother of John Mark, and Lydia of Thyatira, who sold purple cloth, hosted an *ekklēsia*, or assembly, in their homes (Acts 12:12–13; 16:14–15, 40).

PAUL'S AMBIVALENT PERSPECTIVES

Paul wrote the ringing declaration, "There is no longer Jew or Greek, there is no longer slave or free, there is no longer male and female; for all of you are one in Christ Jesus" (Gal 3:28).[39] Yet Paul would invoke customs that insisted upon a subordinate role for women. In 1 Corinthians 11:4–10, he is concerned that women pray or prophesy with their heads covered:

> Any man who prays or prophesies with something on his head disgraces his head, but any woman who prays or prophesies with her head unveiled disgraces her head—it is one and the same thing as having her head shaved. For if a woman will not veil herself, then she should cut off her hair; but if it is disgraceful for a woman to have her hair cut off or to be shaved, she should wear a veil. For a man ought not to have his head veiled, since he is the image and reflection of God; but woman is the reflection of man. Indeed man was not made from woman, but woman from man. Neither was man created for the sake of woman, but woman for the sake of man. For this reason a woman ought to have a symbol of authority on her head, because of the angels.

The meaning of the last verse has long been a conundrum. The text literally says that a woman ought to have *exousia* (power) upon her head on account of the angels. Many interpret *exousia* in the passive sense of a symbol of woman's subjection or of her husband's authority over her. Many likewise accept Gerhard Kittel's interpretation of the word as "veil."[40] In his study on Qumran angelology,[41] Joseph Fitzmyer critiqued Hans Lietzmann's explanation, which invoked the *Testament of Reuben* 5, and said that the veil affords women a magical power of protection against the fallen angels, who were seduced by women in the first place.[42] That interpretation would require the word *angels* (*tous angelous*) to mean bad angels, or angels capable of sinning, which is never the case in Paul.[43] Fitzmyer instead explains the passage according to the Qumran Scrolls, and argues that a woman with her head uncovered is like a person suffering from a bodily defect. Such were never to appear before the angels who assist at gatherings of public worship.[44] Henry Cadbury developed a similar opinion from Dead Sea Scroll material. He maintained that women were considered inherently defective and unclean in Jewish and Essene thought and therefore were to hide themselves from the angels.[45]

Why would the uncovered head of a woman be problematic, especially since Paul himself maintains that her hair is her glory? (1 Cor 11:15). And why "because of the angels?" The influence of the apocryphal or pseudepigraphal myths about fallen angels and women should not be disregarded. The veil was worn as a *symbol* of shame, or a scarlet letter, for once having caused the fall of Adam and of the angels. As will be seen below, Tertullian, in the early third century, will cite the *Book of Enoch* and insist that all women should be veiled as a badge of shame for having caused the fall of the angels.

The motifs found in the pseudepigraphal myths were in the air. In 2 Corinthians 11:3, Paul says that the serpent deceived Eve by his cunning. There was an allusion to the sexual immorality of angels in the Epistle of Jude 6–7. That epistle likewise cites a passage from *Enoch* 1:9 in verses 14–15. There are references to the angels who sinned in 2 Peter 2:4, and to a war in heaven in which Satan and his angels were thrown down to earth (Rev 12:7–9).

Paul seems concerned to maintain traditions and practices that were not prevalent among the gentile Corinthian Christians.[46] He declares that "man was not made from woman, but woman from man. Neither was man created for the sake of woman, but woman for the sake of man." The passage in Genesis 2:20–22, about the first woman being created from Adam's rib, really has no value as a biological fact and does not support a subservient role for women. In the *Summa Theologiae,* Thomas Aquinas discusses the creation of woman from the rib of man and declares it wrong for her to be subject to man's contempt as his slave, because she was not made from his feet (I, q.92, a.3).

Since Paul said that women can pray and prophesy as long as they have their heads covered, some scholars see the passage about women being silent and subordinate in the Church (1 Cor 14:33–35) as a later interpolation, inserted by scribes making copies of Paul's letter.

The First Epistle to Timothy (2:9–15), likely written by a disciple of Paul, explicitly demands woman's submissiveness, arguing from her role in the fall, and further tries to exonerate Adam at the expense of Eve:

> Women should dress themselves modestly and decently in suitable clothing, not with their hair braided, or with gold, pearls, or expensive clothes, but with good works, as is proper for women who profess reverence for God. Let a woman learn in silence with full submission. I permit no woman to teach or to have authority over a man; she is to keep silent. For Adam was formed first, then Eve; and Adam was not deceived, but the woman was deceived and became a transgressor. Yet she will

be saved through childbearing, provided they [women] continue in faith and love and holiness, with modesty.

The concern about jewelry and hair style, also found in the advice given in 1 Peter 3:1–7, intimates that the pseudepigraphal myths may underlie the negative attitude toward women. Such arts were said to be revealed by the fallen watcher angels.

MYTHS RETOLD BY "EARLY CHRISTIAN FATHERS"

Justin Martyr, a Christian philosopher and apologist writing between 150 and 165, explicitly references the watcher theme of *1 Enoch* and *Jubilees*:

> [God] entrusted the care of men and women and of things under heaven to angels whom He appointed over them. But the angels transgressed this order, and were captivated by love of women, and produced children who are called demons. And besides later they enslaved the human race to themselves...and among people they sowed murders, wars, adulteries, intemperate deeds and every evil. (2nd Apology 5:3ff.)[47]

Eve is allegorically presented as the virgin who, having been deceived by Satan, "conceived the word of the serpent and brought forth disobedience and death." By contrast, Mary is the mother of him "by whom God destroys both the serpent and those angels and men who have become like the serpent."[48] The viral and spurious patriarchal prejudices that infected the thinking of Jewish writers now have infected the thinking of early Christian writers.

In the final quarter of the second century, Irenaeus of Lyons alludes to the watcher legend and explicitly mentions Enoch's mission to the angels, but he mainly works with the story of Adam and

Eve's fall in Genesis 3.[49] He includes the embellishments found in the *Apocalypse of Moses* and in the *Life of Adam and Eve*. Satan is a fallen angel whose sin was the refusal to revere man as the image of God. Angry at God, whose order he disobeyed, he is envious of man's lordship over creation.[50] To spite God, Satan seeks to corrupt God's image, man, but can only do it through Eve.[51] Eve is thoroughly deceived by Satan hidden within the serpent and plays into Satan's hands by leading Adam into sin.[52] Eve thus became the cause of death both to herself and to the entire human race.[53] Concupiscence and lust result from the first sin. Adam and Eve previously had had no imagination or conception of what is shameful.[54] Adam, the naive innocent, was caught in the middle of Satan's clash with God and fell only because of Eve's treachery.[55]

Irenaeus systematically exonerates Adam by pushing the blame onto the serpent and his accomplice, Eve.[56] God is said to have interrogated Adam and Eve in order that the blame might fall upon the woman: "He interrogates her that she might convey the blame to the serpent."[57] "But He took compassion upon man, who, through want of care no doubt, but still wickedly [on the part of another], became involved in disobedience; and [God] turned the enmity by which Satan had designed to make [man] the enemy of God, against the author of it, by removing His own anger from man!"[58] As in Justin's *Dialogue*, Mary, by her obedience, brings forth Christ to undo what Eve brought about by her transgression.[59]

In the early third century, Clement of Alexandria likewise tells of the angels who renounced the beauty of God for a beauty that fades. As a result, they fell from heaven to earth, where, having sunk into pleasures, they revealed to women the secrets they knew.[60] In a diatribe against jewelry, Clement complains that certain ornaments used by women are nothing but symbols of adultery, and then makes reference to Eve:

> Yet, these women do not blush when they wear such
> conspicuous symbols of wickedness. Just as the serpent

deceived Eve, so, too, the enticing golden ornament in the shape of a serpent enkindles a mad frenzy in the hearts of the rest of womankind, leading them to have images made of lampreys and snakes as decorations.[61]

While Clement insists, against the Alexandrian Gnostic Julius Cassian, that the marriage act and generation were created by God and are therefore good, he proposes that the circumstances of their first experience were unfortunate. Clement suggests that Adam was prematurely drawn by lust to have relations with Eve so that they were sexually aroused before they should have been. He speculates that the serpent tempted Adam to seek bodily pleasure, like the brute animals, and as a result Adam and Eve conceived before the time scheduled in God's timetable.[62]

Citing Jeremiah 20:14, "Cursed be the day on which I was born![…]let it not be blessed," and Job 14:4–5, "No one is pure from stain, not even if his life is only of one day's duration," Clement intimates that the passages are suggesting that the child has fallen under Adam's curse. Next citing Psalm 51:5, "I was brought into being in sin; my mother conceived me in disobedience to the Law," Clement concludes that David is prophetically speaking of Eve as his mother: "Eve became the mother of all who live (Gen 3:20)."[63] In that perspective, every birth appears related to the sinfulness of the first birth.

In comparison to others of his time, Clement is generally mellow and balanced, with a positive attitude toward life. He seems to have admitted women into his lectures, and he showed appreciation of their equality in nature and their capacity for wisdom (*Strom.* 4, 8, and 19). At the same time, his attitude toward women is colored by fear lest they become sources of sin. Their dresses should not be overly soft and clinging, and should be hemmed below the ankles rather than above the knees—as some young women were apparently wearing them in his time! Women were to wear a veil over their face and a covering over their head, and not circumvent their purpose by wearing purple veils, since colors attract attention and inflame lusts.[64] In a passage discussing attire for church, Clement insists that women be completely veiled except when she is home:

> For her appearance will be dignified only when she cannot be seen. She will never fall into sin if she always keeps modesty before her eyes, and retain her veil, nor will she lure others into an occasion of sin by baring her face. This is what the Word demands, since it is proper for her to pray covered.[65]

In a section on wine-drinking and carousing, Clement declares that woman by her very nature must be concerned with modesty to a much greater degree than is required for a man. "Because her shameless conduct shall not be hid." According to Clement, a woman is quickly drawn into immorality even by only giving consent to pleasure.[66] That woman consistently comes out second best when compared to man is most evident from Clement's discourse on the manliness of beards:

> His head, then, is the badge of a man and shows him unmistakably to be a man. It is older than Eve and is the symbol of the stronger nature. By God's decree, hairiness is one of man's conspicuous qualities, and, at that, hairiness distributed over his whole body. Whatever smoothness or softness there was in him God took from him when he fashioned the delicate Eve from his side to be the receptacle of his seed, his helpmate both in procreation and in the management of the home. What was left (remember, he had lost all traces of hairlessness) was manhood and reveals that manhood. His characteristic is action; hers, passivity. For what is hairy is by nature drier and warmer than what is bare;

therefore, the male is hairier and more warm-blooded than the female; the uncastrated, than the castrated; the mature, than the immature. Thus it is a sacrilege to trifle with the symbol of manhood [the beard].[67]

Origen succeeded Clement as head of the Catechetical School of Alexandria but later moved to Caesarea in Palestine. Influenced by the practice of infant baptism in Palestine, Origen set aside the prenatal fall theory of his earlier *De Principiis* and speculated about the nature of the first sin in terms of the need for purification from uncleanness. Following a line of thinking that is vaguely reminiscent of Clement, Origen believes there is some hidden and secret cause for a woman who has conceived of seed and brought forth to be called "unclean." Citing Psalm 51:5 and Job 14:4–5 as evidence, Origen concludes that her child is also unclean and thus needs baptism.[68] From a passage in his *Commentary on Canticles 3*, the source of such inherent birth pollution might be identified with the theory that Eve was seduced by the serpent, who by his persuasive suggestions poured the poison of sin into her and infected all her posterity. This interpretation would be in line with the *Apocalypse of Moses*.[69] Even when Origen finally returned to a more literal interpretation of Genesis 3 in his *Commentary on Romans* (5,9), he points out that Adam did not know his wife Eve or conceive Cain until after the sin. Finally, in his *Contra Celsum* (6,43), Origen refers to the serpent, who deceived the woman by a promise of divinity.[70] Her example is said to have been followed by the man.

Tertullian was active in Carthage at the turn of the second century. Themes from the apocryphal and pseudepigraphal works of the second and first centuries before Christ appear with full force in both his Catholic and Montanist works. There is no nuanced subtlety about Tertullian's obsession with both virgins and married women wearing veils. In various works, he explains Paul's directive that women at prayer be veiled "on account of the angels" by evoking the sinful union of angels and women from the watcher myth.[71] "It is right that that face which was a snare to them [angels] should wear some mark of a humble guise and obscured beauty" (*Against Marcion* 5, 8).

Tertullian considers the veil a mark of shame for past conduct. This is also evident from a passage in *On the Veiling of Virgins*: "So perilous a face, then, ought to be shaded[...so] that, when standing in the presence of God, at whose bar it stands accused of the driving of the angels from their (native) confines, it may blush before the other angels as well."[72] To justify his preoccupation with the dress and adornment of women, Tertullian refers to Enoch, who taught that women learned about cosmetics and finery from the fallen angels.[73] If God wanted dresses made of purple and scarlet wool, he would have created purple and scarlet sheep. Not only does Tertullian cite Enoch, but, unlike Origen, he treats Enoch as inspired.[74]

Tertullian also intertwines the watcher legend and its demonology with the fall of Adam and Eve in paradise; after the fashion of the later Jewish apocalyptic tradition (*Against Marcion* 5,18), he maintains that the power of the envious angel, the archcorruptor of the universe, has perverted man, the handiwork and image of God. Jealous of man's lordship over creation, the fallen angel wished to establish his own supremacy by corrupting man and, along with him, the entire material world.[75] Unable to launch a frontal attack directly on man, the devil gets at him through Eve. It is she who teaches Adam, who is not yet her husband, what she has learned from the evil one (*De Patientia* 5). Cain is born as a child of wrath sprung from that impatience conceived of the devil's seed with the fertility of evil. Tertullian similarly inserts such allusions about Eve and the devil into an allegorical passage in which Eve is said to believe the serpent as Mary believed Gabriel. The sin that Eve occasioned by believing the devil, Mary wiped away by believing the angel. The devil's word was the seed for Eve so that afterward she gave birth to Cain who murdered his brother; while

Mary bore one who with time would bring salvation to Israel (*De Carne Christi* 17).

For Tertullian, even though the destruction brought about by the female sex was restored to salvation by the same sex, namely Mary, that does not remove the ignominy and the need for expiation on the part of every woman alive:

> No one of you at all, best beloved sisters, from the time that she had first "known the Lord," and learned (the truth) concerning her own (that is, woman's) condition, would have desired too gladsome (not to say too ostentatious) a style of dress; so as not rather to go about in humble garb, and rather to affect meanness of appearance, walking about as Eve mourning and repentant, in order that by every garb of penitence she might the more fully expiate that which she derives from Eve,— the ignominy, I mean, of the first sin, and the odium (attaching to her as the cause) of human perdition. "In pains and anxieties dost thou bear (children), woman; and toward thine husband (is) thy inclination, and he lords it over thee." And do you not know that you are (each) an Eve? The sentence of God on this sex of yours lives in this age: the guilt must of necessity live too. *You* are the devil's gateway; *you* are the unsealer of that (forbidden) tree: *you* are the first deserter of the divine law: *you* are she who persuaded him whom the devil was not valiant enough to attack. *You* destroyed so easily God's image, man. On account of *your* desert[ion]—that is, death—even the Son of God had to die (*De Cultu Feminarum* I, 1).[76]

Unlike Tertullian, Augustine rejected *tales* such as the watcher myth (*De Civitate Dei* 15, 23) and considered the *Book of Enoch* to be apocryphal. But some of the motifs developed in later

Jewish apocalyptic literature may have influenced his hypothesis that original sin is transmitted from parent to child through the concupiscence or lust that is a result of the first sin and accompanies the act of generation.[77]

AN ABIDING NEGATIVE ATTITUDE TOWARD WOMEN

The myths discussed above no longer circulated in later centuries, but a negative mindset regarding women persisted. For example, consider canon 813 of the 1917 Code of Canon Law:

§1. A priest should not celebrate Mass without a minister who assists him and responds.

§2. The minister serving at Mass should not be a woman unless, in the absence of a man, for a just cause, under the condition that the woman respond from a distance and in no way approach the altar.[78]

In 1949, just thirteen years before the Second Vatican Council, the Congregation for the Discipline of the Sacraments issued an Instruction on Domestic Chapels, such as in convents of sisters or cloistered nuns. It reiterated the ban on women approaching the altar, and stated that all authors unanimously declare that it was a mortal sin (*sub mortali prohibitum*) for a woman to approach the altar![79]

Such diminishment of women contrasts sharply with what Acts of the Apostles (2:42–46) tells about the early disciples: "They devoted themselves to the apostles' teaching and fellowship [*koinonia*], to the breaking of bread and prayers." They broke bread in homes. In Jerusalem, many had gathered and were praying in the house of Mary, the mother of John Mark (Acts 12:12). In Philippi, disciples gathered in the home of Lydia, a dealer in purple cloth, who was from the city of Thyatira (Acts 16:11–15, 40). Imagine telling Mary or Lydia to stand away from the table where "the breaking of bread" was celebrated.

On January 10, 2021, Pope Francis issued *Spiritus Domini* ("Spirit of the Lord"), his *motu proprio* Apostolic Letter that modified canon 230 §1. The church law that previously referred only to "lay men" was changed to read,

> *Lay persons* who possess the age and qualifications established by decree of the conference of bishops can be admitted on a stable basis through the prescribed liturgical rite to the ministries of lector and acolyte.[80]

Pope Francis specified that he welcomed recommendations coming from various synodal assemblies, writing that "a doctrinal development has taken place in recent years which has highlighted how certain ministries instituted by the Church are based on the common condition of being baptized and the royal priesthood received in the Sacrament of Baptism."

In 1 Corinthians 11:7–9, Paul maintained a notion drawn from Genesis 2: man alone was made in the image of God; woman was derived from the rib of Adam and made for him. Therefore, woman was considered subordinate because of her very mode of creation. A very different perspective was presented in the *retold* creation narrative in Genesis 1. It proclaimed, "God created humankind in his image, in the image of God he created them; male and female he created them." Persons, men and women *together*, are the image of God. Altar girls and altar boys!

6

CAN ORDINATION ONLY FOR MEN REALLY BE DECLARED DIVINELY REVEALED?

JESUS CHOSE THE Twelve to "sit on (twelve) thrones judging the twelve tribes of Israel" (Matt 19:28; Luke 22:28–30). He emphasized service, but did not otherwise predetermine the development of the community coming from him. After his death and resurrection there were no specific leadership structures in place beyond the Twelve. And there is no evidence that Jesus provided the early Church with a detailed blueprint offering specific directions.

In the fifties and sixties, we find the work: of Peter and Paul; of Phoebe, "a benefactor of many," called "deacon" of the church at Cenchreae; of Prisca and Aquila who traveled with Paul (Acts 18:18, 26) and in whose home in Rome an *ekklēsia* gathered; of Mary who also "worked very hard" in Rome; and of Andronicus and Junia (or Julia) "prominent among the apostles" (Rom 16:1–7). There were likely many others, such as the companions of Paul, mentioned in Acts 20:4, who joined in proclaiming the risen Lord and serving Spirit-filled churches in the time after the resurrection.

Raymond Brown has shown that the high Christology of the community of the Fourth Gospel, in which the Word become flesh manifests his glory, allowed it to place less emphasis on leadership structures than the congregations reflected in other Gospels.[1] The Community of the Beloved Disciple was united in the loving relationship of its members to a Jesus who served and who left a command of love (John 13:1–35): "If I…have washed your feet, you also ought to wash one another's feet.…you also should do as I have done to you" (John 13:14–15). Jesus is the vine and his followers are the branches who live in him by their love: "love one another as I have loved you" (John 15:1–12). "I have called you friends, because I have made known to you everything that I have heard from my Father" (John 15:15). Even Peter's postresurrection role is likewise related to his love for Jesus (21:15–17).

Matthew, Luke/Acts, and the later "deutero-Pauline" tradition (in the Epistles to Timothy and Titus) placed greater emphasis on structures of authority and leadership, which produced communities more sociologically stable than those reflected by the Johannine Epistles.

The development of the earliest churches involved a diversity of leadership patterns. Philippi had a collegial group of overseers (*episkopoi*) and deacons (*diakonoi*) (Phil 1:2). Jerusalem had the Twelve; James the brother of the Lord (Gal 1:19), with a collegial group of elders (*presbyteroi*); and the Seven, leaders for Hellenistic Jewish followers of Jesus (Acts 6:1–6; 15:4–6, 22; 21:18). Antioch had prophets and teachers who could be sent out on a missionary journey, as were Barnabas and Saul (Acts 13:1–3). Corinth originally worked with the gifts or charisms of members of the community (1 Cor 12:27–31).

In the eighties, the collegial structures of elders and overseers, but now interchangeably known as elders/overseers, proliferated across churches, including Corinth (Acts 20:17, 28; 1 Tim 3:1–7; 5:17–19; *1 Clement* 42, 44). In the early second century, the letters of Ignatius of Antioch presented a tripartite structure of one *episkopos* (or bishop), with an advisory council of elders (*presbyteroi*), and a group of deacons. Ignatius declares, "Without these (a mono-*episkopos*, elders, and deacons) no gathering can be called an *ekklēsia* or church" (*Trallians* 3). That would become the standard pattern in every church.

Ignatius presumed that the entire *ekklēsia* or assembly *does* or *makes* the Eucharist, but he insisted that a valid Eucharist is presided over by the *episkopos* or one to whom he entrusts that role (*Smyrnaeans* 8). No one was to do anything pertaining to an *ekklēsia* apart from its *episkopos* or bishop. For Ignatius, the local assembly, united under its bishop, made the universal Church present in that place: "Wherever the bishop appears, there the people should be, just as wherever Jesus is, there is the universal [catholic] assembly [*katholikē ekklēsia*]" (*Smyr.* 8:2).

For Ignatius, the bishop was the figure (*tupon*) of God the Father. The presbyters or elders were likened to the council of God and college of apostles (*Magnesians* 6; *Trallians* 3). They were advisors to the bishop and did not universally assume a eucharistic role until the fifth century. The deacons were revered for being servants like Jesus.

In the early decades of the *ekklēsia*, those who held positions of leadership were married men with families (1 Tim 3:1–15; Titus 1:5–6). As Paul declared, "Do we not have the right to be accompanied by a believing [sister] wife [woman], as do the other apostles and the brothers of the Lord and Cephas [Peter]" (1 Cor 9:5). Such relationships with women gradually disappeared as disciplinary laws began to impose continence and celibacy during the fourth century.[2] In western churches of the fifth and sixth centuries, there were still many married bishops who had raised families. Augustine sent a loaf of bread, a symbolic gift of unity (*koinonia*), with his letter (31:9) to Paulinus, bishop of Nola in Campania, and his wife, Therasia.[3] Augustine, now a bishop, had previously received a loaf from Paulinus and Therasia.[4] In the thirteenth century, Bonaventure's *Rule for Novices* declared, "Flee from the company of women, as you would from serpents. Never speak with a woman, unless urgent necessity compels you, and never look at the face of any woman. If any woman speaks with you cut her off as quickly as possible [*swiftly kill her words*]."[5] In a celibate, clerical world, women would be characterized as temptations or sources of sin.

In the first century, Mary and Lydia hosted an *ekklēsia* or assembly in their homes (Acts 12:12–13; 16:14–15, 40). But, in the third century, the church order document called the *Didascalia*, written in Syria, restricted the term *laity* to male members of the church with economic status. They were to support widows and orphans and to honor the deacons, elders, and bishop with gifts (2.28). Their "honoraria" financially supported the bishop's work and his care for the needy and strangers (2.24–36). Women had an active role as deaconesses and were to be honored by the people in the place of the Holy Spirit (*Didascalia* 2.26). But their ministry was very much circumscribed. They could visit and minister to sick women in their homes and perform the baptismal anointings of women for the bishop (3.12), but they could not baptize. Women who were not deaconesses or officially appointed members of the order of widows (3.1–2) were to be subject to their husbands (1.8) and were to sit "apart" in the assembly for the Eucharist (2.57). On the street, women were to cover their face with a veil and to walk looking downward (1.8, 10).

During the fourth century, Basil of Caesarea taught that, by custom, a wife who was regularly beaten ought to endure it rather than be separated from her husband (Ep. 188.9). Augustine praised his mother because she counseled women with battered faces not to criticize the husbands that beat them. Monica's "joking" advice, that women should view marriage as a contract for making them slaves (*Confessions* 9,9), seems appalling in the present sociocultural context.

An effort to enable women to dedicate their lives to God through active service within society especially emerged during the sixteenth century. In 1535, Angela Merici brought together a "company" of women under the patronage of St. Ursula, to work for the revitalization of family life in their native Brescia. They intended to live under a rule that "was the first in the Western

Church drawn up for women by a woman," with no habit, no cloister, and a private vow of chastity.[6] But the bishops under whom they worked had different ideas. In 1546 the bishop of Brescia required them to wear a simple habit. After their spread to Milan, Cardinal Charles Borromeo imposed further conditions. Thereafter, the women went out only with permission and no longer taught in homes but only within the community. The most extreme modifications came during the "company's" spread into France, where Angela's group of apostolic women living and working in the family circle was finally transformed into the cloistered nuns known as the Ursulines. The expectations of the time, that women should be either married or cloistered but certainly not "freelance charitable workers," eventually prevailed.

In 1610, Francis de Sales, as bishop of Geneva, founded a community of women with simple vows living in a flexible cloister, which would allow the "daughters of the Visitation" the freedom to do external works of charity for the needy. But, since visiting the sick and teaching children, particularly boys, were not considered suitable tasks for consecrated virgins, they too were eventually forced into a totally cloistered life.

To avoid a similar fate for his Daughters of Charity, begun in 1633, Vincent de Paul insisted that they were not "religious" or a "congregation." They would have no grille or enclosure, but only regulations about contact on the streets. They took private vows and wore no religious garb or veil but adopted the ordinary gray serge dress worn by young women in the area around Paris. Instead of having a chaplain, they prayed and confessed in their local parish. When their private rule was officially approved by the Archbishop of Paris in 1646, the matter of clerical supervision was specifically spelled out for the future. But the Daughters of Charity managed to escape the cloister and soon added the ministry of teaching to their care of the sick.[7]

Earlier, Mary Ward had founded the Institute of the English Ladies at St. Omer in France with the bold idea of establishing schools for girls the way the Jesuits had for boys.[8] Rather than using a rule approved for nuns, in 1611 her community adapted the rule of the Jesuits and wore the ordinary dress of the time. Although the bishop of St. Omer defended them, many others expressed outrage and shock. A group of English clerics complained to Pope Gregory XV, arguing that women had never undertaken an apostolic office in the Church and that the present was no time to begin. Stereotyping the female sex as "soft, flexible, slippery, inconstant, erroneous, always grasping for novelties, and subject to a thousand dangers," the clerics concluded that women should not be living outside a cloister.[9]

Having already requested Rome's approval, Ward personally presented her case there in 1621 and 1624, asking for papal recognition that would prevent the interference of bishops, an innovation never previously considered for women. Rome's approval never came because the Ladies would not give up their apostolate and stay in their convents to pray, and because they refused to wear a habit. After founding new institutes in Italy, Ward did the same in Munich, until three clerics from the Holy Office arrived there and imprisoned her in a convent. She was freed through the intervention of Pope Urban VIII, but the opposition prevailed and her Institute was officially suppressed in 1631. It survived only in Munich and, remarkably, in Rome, where it continued under the personal invitation of the pope.

Although Ward's initiatives were ahead of her time and were thus considered too revolutionary, they ultimately contributed to the gradual recognition (in papal documents dated 1706, 1749, and finally 1889, 1900, and 1901)[10] of religious communities of "sisters." Unlike "nuns," "sisters" would not be cloistered, and were thereby free to exercise a public apostolate. The earlier insistence on a permanent enclosure or cloister was reshaped into a plethora of directives imposing a kind of portable cloister. Until Vatican II, in order to obtain recognition as religious, congregations of women usually had to accept the imposition of the religious habit and veil, rules regarding contact with others, and detailed regulations regarding the use of parlors for visitors, the need for sister companions, and the avoidance of contact with strangers via "custody of the eyes" on the street.

At the first and second sessions of the Second Vatican Council, there was not one woman among the almost three thousand participants. A select group of male auditors had been invited; but no women were at the sessions in 1962 and 1963. On September 21, 1964, on the initiative of Pope Paul VI, twenty-three women were invited to be auditors at the Council for the first time in history. Most were religious sisters, but there was only one married woman. Carmel McEnroy has chronicled their experience and reflections in *Guests in Their Own House.*[11]

A *NEW* QUESTION: CAN WOMEN BE ORDAINED TO THE PRIESTLY MINISTRY?

Women have assumed ever more significant roles in the Church. Religious and "lay" women, with degrees in theology, liturgical studies, pastoral ministry, and religious education have made enormous contributions in service to the Church. Some women sought a more significant ministerial role. The *Commentary* issued by the Congregation for the Doctrine of Faith on October 15, 1976, provides a timeline.[12] In September 1958, the Swedish Lutheran Church was the first to admit women to pastoral office. That initiative is said to have gradually spread among the Reformed Churches "which denied the sacramentality of Orders" when they separated from the Church of Rome. Then, in 1971 and 1973 the Anglican Bishop of Hong Kong ordained three women with the agreement of his Synod. In July 1974, the episcopal bishop of Philadelphia ordained eleven women to the priesthood, which was afterward declared invalid by the House of Bishops. Rome took notice since these ordinations occurred in assemblies that claimed to have preserved the apostolic succession of Orders. In June 1975, the General Synod of the Anglican Church in Canada approved the principle of women being ordained to the priesthood. In a letter dated July 9, 1975, the Archbishop of Canterbury, Frederick D. Coggan, apprised Pope Paul VI "of the slow but steady growth of a consensus of opinion within the Anglican Communion that there are no fundamental objections in principle to the ordination of women to the priesthood."[13] (An Italian translation was published in *L'Osservatore Romano* on September 2, 1975.) Those developments generated statements of nonacceptance from the pope and others in the leadership of the Roman Catholic Church and from the Eastern Orthodox Churches.

THE RESPONSE OF THE PONTIFICAL BIBLICAL COMMISSION

In April 1976, the Pontifical Biblical Commission convened, being asked "to study the role of women in the Bible in the course of research to determine the place that could be given to women in the church. The question for which an answer was especially sought was whether or not women could be ordained to the priestly ministry (especially as ministers of the eucharist [Mass] and as leaders of the Christian community)."[14] The members of the Commission were eminent biblical scholars, all priests, appointed by the pope. In their report, they noted that the role of women does not constitute the principal subject of biblical texts. Even more significantly, they declared that the formulation of the question that they were charged to study—the priesthood, the celebrant of the Eucharist, and leadership of the local community—was a way of looking at things that is somewhat foreign to the Bible. The New Testament never uses the term *priest* (*hiereus* in Greek) in relation to Christian ministry or the Eucharist. A eucharistic priesthood is a later conception, now being broadened in recent church teachings.

After an analysis of the situation of women during the ministry of Jesus and in the earliest decades of the Church, as found in the Acts of the Apostles and the Letters of Paul, the Commission *unanimously* declared, "It does not seem that the New Testament by itself alone will permit us to settle in a clear way and once and for all the problem of the possible accession of women to the presbyterate." On the question whether scriptural grounds alone are *not* enough to exclude the ordination of women, the vote was twelve yes, five no. On whether ordaining women would *not* contravene Christ's plan, the vote was again twelve yes to five no.[15] Such positions of the Biblical Commission scholars were considered merely advisory and did not find reception in the Vatican.

THE DECLARATION *INTER INSIGNIORES*

The Congregation for the Doctrine of Faith, then headed by Cardinal Franjo Šeper, met in the fall of that same year. It produced its declaration *Inter Insigniores* on the Question of the Admission of Women to the Ministerial Priesthood, which was approved by Pope Paul VI and officially issued on October 15, 1976.[16] The Introduction (par. 6) acknowledges, "We are dealing with a debate which classical theology scarcely touched upon." But the Congregation "judges it necessary to recall that the Church, in fidelity to the example of the Lord, does not consider herself authorized to admit women to priestly ordination." And "deems it opportune at the present juncture to explain this position of the Church" (par. 5).

Section 1 (par. 6) states that "the Catholic Church has never felt that priestly or episcopal ordination can be validly conferred on women." It acknowledges "that in the writings of the Fathers one will find the undeniable influence of prejudices unfavorable to women," but then questionably asserts "it should be noted that these prejudices had hardly any influence on their pastoral activity, and still less on their spiritual direction."[17] Invoking the canonical documents of the Antiochian and Egyptian tradition, it concludes "that by calling only men to the priestly Order and ministry in its true sense, the Church intends to remain faithful to the type of ordained ministry *willed by the Lord Jesus Christ* and carefully maintained by the Apostles" (par. 6). The Magisterium, over the centuries, "has not felt the need to intervene in order to formulate a principle which was not attacked, or to defend a law which was not challenged" (par. 8).

Section 2 (par. 10) denies any influence of culture. Jesus is said to have deliberately not called any women to be among the Twelve. It insists that he purposefully did that, and not to conform to the customs of his time. Discussing Jesus's interactions with women, the document notes that they were charged by the risen Jesus to take the first paschal message to the apostles "in order to prepare the latter to become the official witnesses to the Resurrection" (par. 12). It acknowledges that such facts about the role of women "do not make the matter immediately obvious." It argues that the Word of God goes beyond the obvious. The ultimate meaning of Jesus's mission and the ultimate meaning of Scripture cannot be reached by a purely historical exegesis of the text. It instead invokes "a number of convergent indications." It argues that Jesus intentionally excluded women, since he didn't make his mother an apostle (par. 13)!

In note 10, the Congregation discounts the Q passage (Matt 19:25; Luke 22:30) in which Jesus relates the Twelve sitting on twelve thrones to the twelve tribes of Israel. It instead invokes Mark 3:14: "He appointed twelve, whom he also named apostles, to be with him, and to be sent out to proclaim the message." Raymond Brown has questioned that substitution: "These words (which are the words of Mark and not of Jesus) tell us how Mark understood the role of the Twelve; they most certainly may not be used to overrule the words of Jesus himself in determining 'the attitude of Christ' toward the Twelve." Mark 3:14 was invoked to maintain that "the Twelve represent Jesus to the people and carry on his work." It was used to buttress the Congregation's conclusion that "Jesus did not entrust the apostolic charge to women" (par. 13). Brown comments, "Fortunately it is a firm principle in theology that loyal acceptance of a Roman document does not require that one approve the reasons offered."[18]

Section 4 (par. 18) begins by asking, "Could the Church today depart from this attitude of Jesus and the Apostles, which has been considered as normative by the whole of tradition up to our own day"? The Congregation asserts that it could not do that, repeatedly insisting that it is God's plan that women cannot be ordained. It argues that the directive in 1 Corinthians 14:34–35 and 1 Timothy 2:12 imposing silence and submission on women "solely concerns the official function of teaching in the Christian assembly." Citing 1 Corinthians 11:7 and Genesis 2:18–24, which tell of woman being created after man, it claims that Paul considers the prescription of silence "bound up with the divine plan of creation. It would be difficult to see in it the expression of a cultural fact" (par. 20).

Given that God creates by means of a 13.8-billion-year process of evolution, the narrative about God creating Adam and then creating the first woman from Adam's rib is questionably invoked as justification for imposing silence and submission on women. The core of the creation narrative in Genesis 2 is that God created humans and that the woman was to be a *partner* (Gen 2:18) for the man. The description of the manner in which the first woman was created reflects patriarchal imagination. The later priestly creation narrative simply said, "So God created humankind in his image, in the image of God he created them; male and female he created them" (Gen 1:27).

The Congregation's argumentation next turned to the limits of the Church's power over the sacraments, particularly regarding the substance of the sacraments. The Church is said to decide what can change and what must remain immutable because the Church "is bound by Christ's manner of acting" (par. 23). The practice of the Church is said to have a normative character: "in the fact of conferring priestly ordination only on men, it is a question of an unbroken tradition throughout the history of the Church, universal in the East and the West....This norm, based on Christ's example, has been and is still observed because it is considered to conform to God's plan for his Church" (par. 24).

Intending to "clarify" why only men have been called to priestly ordination, the Congregation turns to the notion first introduced in the third century by Cyprian of Carthage, that the priest (*sacerdos*), which then meant the *episkopos* or bishop, presided at the altar table in the place of Christ, *vice Christi* (Epistle 63, 14). In celebrating the Eucharist, the priest acts not only through the effective power conferred on him by Christ, but in the person of Christ, taking on the role of Christ (par. 26). Citing Thomas Aquinas that "sacramental signs represent what they signify by natural resemblance," the Congregation insists that the same natural resemblance is required for persons, which would not be the case if the role of Christ were not taken by a man. Christ's role as a person must be taken by a man (par. 27). "Christ is the bridegroom; the Church is his bride" (par. 29). "That is why we can never ignore the fact that Christ is a man" (par. 30).

Inter Insigniores acknowledged that the priest also acts *in persona ecclesiae*, in the person of the Church, and asked, "Would it not be possible to think that this representation could be carried out by a woman?" That idea was immediately declared to be inseparable from Cyprian's notion that the presider at the altar table acts in the place of Christ, *vice Christi* (Epistle 63): "It is precisely because he first represents Christ himself, who is the Head and Shepherd of the Church" (par. 32).

An educated rhetorician, Cyprian became a Christian soon after 245 and was elected as bishop of Carthage sometime before Easter of 249, amid resentment by more senior presbyters. At the end of that year, Decius became emperor of Rome and issued a decree that all inhabitants of the empire were to receive certificates (*libelli*) that they had offered sacrifice to the gods of Rome. Cyprian went into hiding. During the persecution that followed, Christians, who did not have Cyprian's self-seclusion as an option, *witnessed* to their faith by suffering imprisonment or torture as "confessors," or by their death as martyrs. But many became *lapsed* Christians, who offered a ceremonial sacrifice to the gods of Rome (with some acting as proxies for many). A number found a way to purchase *libelli* without sacrificing.[19]

When Cyprian returned from his self-imposed exile, he objected to the practice of the confessor Lucian who had been distributing *libelli pacis*, certificates of peace or forgiveness, to large numbers of Christians, readmitting those who had participated in the sacrifices back into communion with the Church.[20] Lucian reconciled the lapsed by presiding at the Eucharist and giving them communion. That practice was justified by the martyr tradition preserved in the *Apostolic Tradition*, 9, that a confessor, who had been imprisoned in chains, shall not have hands laid on him for the order of deacons or the order of presbyters, because he has the honor of the presbyterate by his confession.[21] Claiming a bond with martyred confessors, Lucian extended their self-sacrifice to absolve Christians whose witness had failed in the persecution.[22]

Cyprian contended that only he, as bishop, had the prerogative to reconcile the lapsed, and that had to be done by his imposition of hands.[23] Cyprian also declared that confessors had to have hands imposed if they were to be made presbyters or deacons.[24] The confessor was therefore no longer recognized as having a self-authenticating ministry. Cyprian insisted, "It is the great honor of our episcopate...to grant peace to the martyrs."[25]

Cyprian further devised a strategy to claim the status of confessor for himself.[26] He appropriated the image of martyr as *sacerdos* to that of bishop (*episkopos*) as *sacerdos*. As Allen Brent has shown, Cyprian drew his theology of the priest-bishop as imitator of Christ at the Eucharist from the cult of the martyrs:[27] "For if Christ Jesus...is himself the great high priest [*summus sacerdos*]... and if he offered himself as a sacrifice to the Father...and directed that this should be done in remembrance of him, then without doubt a priest truly serves in Christ's place (*vice Christi*) who imitates what Christ did, and offers up a true and complete sacrifice."[28] Cyprian shifted the suffering and absolving Christ from the face of the martyr onto the face of the priest-bishop.

Cyprian focused on establishing his episcopal authority over against those practicing ecclesial reconciliation independent of his oversight. His strategy was directed against *men* who claimed the presbyterate as confessors in the persecution. He thus devised the idea that the presider of the Eucharist acts *vice Christi* as defensive tactic of his authority that involved an element of self-aggrandizement. The New Testament never uses the term *hiereus*, priest, in relation to the Eucharist. Nor is any individual identified as acting *vice Christi*. In the second century, Ignatius of Antioch said that a valid Eucharist is presided over by the bishop or one whom he appoints, but Ignatius associated himself to God the Father: his advisory council of presbyters was compared to the apostles. The deacons were likened to Jesus, because they *served* the needs of the assembly.[29] But Cyprian's new claim of serving in Christ's place (*vice Christi*) at the Eucharist found acceptance in the hierarchical milieu of the ensuing centuries. It has now been invoked by *Inter Insigniores* in response to a totally new question.

It should be noted that there were also women confessors in Cyprian's era. Eusebius, in his *History of the Church*, tells of Blandina, a woman repeatedly tortured in a persecution in Lyons in 177. Hung on a post and exposed as food for the wild beasts let loose in the arena, "she appeared to be hanging cross wise, and… those undergoing their ordeal, saw in the appearance of their sister him who was crucified for them…a small weak, despised woman who had put on Christ."[30] Her fellow Christians saw Christ in her.

"The logic of ordination through martyrdom, it can be argued, failed through social prejudice in the case of women, but nevertheless remained potent, as Cyprian was to find, in the case of men."[31] Given the cultural presuppositions of the third century, Cyprian did not give attention to women like Blandina who imitated and "put on Christ." He strategized with much effort against *male* confessors acting independently of his authority. He shifted the suffering and absolving Christ from the face of the martyr onto the face of the priest-bishop who "serves in Christ's place (*vice Christi*) who imitates what Christ did, and offers up a true and complete sacrifice."[32] Removed from its original context, the passage about serving "in Christ's place [*vice Christi*]" at the Eucharist has now been invoked by *Inter Insigniores* to buttress the exclusion of women. Given the culture of our time, think about transferring Cyprian's third-century tactic, from his face as priest-bishop to the face of an ordained woman who *imitates and puts on Christ*.

In a sixth, concluding section, the laying on of hands is said to guarantee God's choice: "It is the Holy Spirit, given by ordination, who grants participation in the ruling power of the Supreme Pastor, Christ" (par. 35). Paul's declaration that "there is no longer male and female; for all of you are one in Christ Jesus" (Gal 3:28–29) is said to "not concern ministries…baptism does not confer any personal title to public ministry in the Church" (par. 35).

Noting that some women are said to feel a vocation to the priesthood, the Declaration responds that "the priesthood does not form part of the rights of the individual….The priestly office cannot become the goal of social advancement" (par. 38). The Church is said to be "a differentiated body, in which each individual has his or her role. The roles are distinct, and must not be confused" (par. 39).

KARL RAHNER'S ASSESSMENT OF *INTER INSIGNIORES*

In "Women and the Priesthood," Rahner reflected on the declaration and "the question of the possibility or non-possibility of the ordination of women."[33] Limiting his analysis to the theological aspect, he excluded questions "from a secular anthropology of the sexes, from the history of civilization, from an analysis of modern society with its demand for equality of the sexes, and so on."[34] Rahner notes the declaration's emphasis on "constant tradition," and its conclusion that Jesus "intended in principle to exclude women from the priestly ministry for all times and under all sociological conditions, although it is admitted that a purely historical exegesis of the texts of Scripture does not 'make the matter immediately obvious.'"

Turning to the theological qualification of the declaration, Rahner acknowledges that, independently of the proposed arguments, it has a certain weight as a statement of the Roman authorities on faith. "Nevertheless, despite papal approval, the Declaration is not a definitive decision; it is in principle reformable and it can (that is not to say *a priori* that it must) be erroneous."[35] Its appeal to an uninterrupted tradition is not necessarily an appeal to a definitively binding tradition. Giving it the respect that it deserves, the theologian has the right and duty of critically examining it "even to the point of regarding it as objectively erroneous in its basic thesis...there is a whole series of declarations of the Roman authorities on faith which have meanwhile been shown to be erroneous or at least largely obsolete."[36]

Rahner goes on to assess the essential argument of the declaration: "that the practice of Jesus and the Apostles, which makes no suggestion of the ordination of women to the priesthood, cannot be explained in the light of the sociological and cultural situation at the time." The declaration assumes an intention on the part of Jesus that is not historically and sociologically conditioned: "it holds for all times and must be respected faithfully by the Church at all times."[37] It asserts that Jesus (and up to a point, also Paul) were "completely opposed to the depreciation of women at the time and thus could have spoken out against the exclusion of women from positions of leadership" yet also admits "that some of Paul's ordinances on the behaviour of women are influenced by 'the customs of the period' and therefore 'no longer have normative value.'"[38]

The declaration's argumentation is likewise defective in its overly simple suppositions about the transition from the concept of the apostle and the Twelve to the concept of the priest (and bishop). That does not fit in with our present-day knowledge of the origins, structure, and organization of the primitive Church. "The Declaration leaves out all the difficult questions about the concrete emergence of the Church and its origins from Jesus, although they are of the greatest importance for its theme." Given that, Rahner asks whether it is possible "to deduce from Jesus' choice of men for the college of the Twelve any definite and unambiguous conclusions with regard to the question of an ordinary, simple leader of the community and president [presider] of the eucharistic celebration in a particular congregation of a later period."[39] Is it possible to look at all to Jesus and the apostles for a plan regarding the structure of communities?

The declaration seems to restrict the proper function of the priest to the sacramental power of consecration: "We almost get the impression that the Declaration would be prepared to concede to women practically all ecclesiastical functions except this one (and 'the official and public proclamation of the message,' which hardly seems consistent with Jesus' commission to the women [Matt 28:10]...to take the first paschal message to the Apostles themselves)."[40]

Rahner observes that "Judaism in Jesus' time (as is clearly noticeable still in Paul's writings) was based on a male domination so much taken for granted that it is quite impossible to think that Jesus and his Apostles (and with them their Hellenistic congregations under the influence of Judaism) could have abolished or even have been permitted to abolish this male preponderance in their congregations." Given the cultural and sociological perspectives on women at that time, "there would have been considerable resistance...to the appointment of women as leaders in the congregations." There would have been even stronger resistance in setting up female congregational leaders as presiders of the eucharistic celebration. But "the question must be considered from the standpoint of leadership in the congregation and not from that of strictly sacramental powers," given that "there is no immediate evidence of a special power over the Eucharist anywhere in the New Testament."[41] As noted above, the Pontifical Biblical Commission similarly declared that the idea of priesthood as the celebrant of the Eucharist and leader of the local community is a way of looking at things that is somewhat foreign to the Bible. A eucharistic priesthood is a later conception.

The declaration maintains that the existing cultural and sociological situation was not the reason why Jesus and the apostles did not appoint women to positions of leadership but is completely silent about any alternate reasons. "The mere fact that Jesus was of the male sex is no answer here, since it is not clear that a person acting with Christ's mandate and in that sense (but not otherwise) *in persona Christi* must at the same time represent Christ precisely in his *maleness*."[42] An appeal to the "divine order of creation" would compromise the declaration's recognition of the equal rights and dignity of women.

Rahner concludes that theology must continue its reflections. The Roman declaration says that in the question of women and the priesthood, the Church must remain faithful to Jesus Christ. "But what fidelity means in connection with this problem remains an open question. Consequently the discussion must continue...but also with that courage for historical change which is part of the fidelity which the Church owes to its Lord."[43]

EVADING AND PROHIBITING FURTHER DISCUSSION: AUTHORITARIAN TACTICS

In 1994, Pope John Paul II issued an Apostolic Letter, *Ordinatio Sacerdotalis* (Priestly Ordination), addressed to all bishops.[44] It stated, "Priestly ordination, which hands on the office entrusted by Christ to his Apostles of teaching, sanctifying and governing the faithful, has in the Catholic Church from the beginning always been reserved to men alone. This tradition has also been faithfully maintained by the Oriental Churches." The letter declares that the declaration issued by the Congregation for the Doctrine of the Faith had concluded that the Church "does not consider herself authorized to admit women to priestly ordination." The declaration is also said to offer "theological reasons which illustrate the appropriateness of the divine provision," and show clearly "that Christ's way of acting did not proceed from sociological or cultural motives peculiar to his time....The real reason is that, in giving the Church her fundamental constitution, her theological anthropology—thereafter always followed by the Church's Tradition—Christ established things in this way."

John Paul recalls that, in his previous Apostolic Letter *Mulieris Dignitatem* (On the Dignity and Vocation of Women), issued in 1988, he had written, "In calling only men as his Apostles, Christ acted in a completely free and sovereign manner. In doing so, he exercised the same freedom with which, in all his behaviour, he emphasized the dignity and the vocation of women, without conforming to the prevailing customs and to the traditions sanctioned by the legislation of the time."

The fact that Jesus's mother, Mary, "received neither the mission proper to the Apostles nor the ministerial priesthood" is said to show clearly that the nonadmission of women to priestly ordination cannot mean that women are of lesser dignity, nor can it be construed as discrimination against them. Rather, it is to be seen as the faithful observance of a plan to be ascribed to the wisdom of the Lord of the universe. The presence and role of women in the lie and ministry of the Church is declared "absolutely necessary and irreplaceable," although not linked to the ministerial priesthood.

Pope John Paul II's letter did not ask or discuss whether the long and undisputed practice of not ordaining women rests on a divine plan or revelation or whether it could represent a human tradition rooted in past societal norms and roles that need not be permanent.[45] He simply declares, "In giving the Church her fundamental constitution, her theological anthropology...Christ established things in this way"; "Christ acted in a completely free and sovereign manner…without conforming to the prevailing customs and to the traditions sanctioned by the legislation of the time;" "the non-admission of women to priestly ordination is…to be seen as the faithful observance of a plan to be ascribed to the wisdom of the Lord of the universe." It is "a matter which pertains to the Church's divine constitution itself."

The final section of *Ordinatio Sacerdotalis* makes clear that its purpose was to close off analysis and discussion of such questions:

> Although the teaching that priestly ordination is to be reserved to men alone has been preserved by the constant and universal Tradition of the Church and firmly taught by the Magisterium in its more recent documents, at the present time in some places it is nonetheless considered still open to debate, or the Church's judgment that women are not to be admitted to ordination is considered to have a merely disciplinary force.
>
> Wherefore, in order that all doubt may be removed regarding a matter of great importance, a matter which pertains to the Church's divine constitution itself, in virtue of my ministry of confirming the brethren (cf. Lk 22:32) I declare that the Church has no authority whatsoever to confer priestly ordination on women and that this judgment is to be definitively held by all the Church's faithful.

The wording of the final sentence, "that the Church has no authority whatsoever to confer priestly ordination on women and *that this judgment is to be definitively held* by all the Church's faithful" applies a distinction found in the documentation of the First Vatican Council. The record indicates that Vatican I did not intend to declare that the pope could be infallible about *any* issue confronted by the Church, but only about revealed truths or those closely related to revelation. Speaking for the Deputation of Faith, entrusted with the consideration of amendments proposed during the conciliar debates, Bishop Gasser declared that the object of infallibility extended to truths that constitute "the deposit of faith," and also to truths not revealed but "requisite for maintaining the integrity of the deposit of revelation." He went on to clarify that it is not a dogma "of divine and catholic faith" but rather "theologically certain" that the pope is infallible about matters that were not revealed but necessary for defending and explaining the faith.[46] This qualification was reflected in a change in the final draft of the canon defining papal infallibility. It dropped an earlier reference exacting the assent of *faith* (*de fide tenendum*) and simply said that what the pope teaches must be held (*tenendam*) by the universal Church.[47] Teachings connected to Revelation are to be believed (*credenda*); teachings that do not have an explicit connection to Revelation are to be held (*tenenda*). Pope John Paul's teaching that women cannot be ordained must be definitively *held* (*tenenda*), rather than believed (*credenda*). It is a definitive teaching that does not presently call for the response of faith but rather for *obedient reception of* the papal decree. One must also keep in mind that, although what is "defined" is "irreformable," the possibility of further clarification or the perfectibility of what was defined was not excluded.[48]

On October 28, 1995, the Congregation for the Doctrine of the Faith, then headed by Cardinal Joseph Ratzinger as Prefect, published a response to a question (*dubium*) concerning the teaching contained in *Ordinatio Sacerdotalis*:

> Whether the teaching that the Church has no authority whatsoever to confer priestly ordination on women, which is presented in the Apostolic Letter *Ordinatio Sacerdotalis* to be held definitively, is to be understood as pertaining to the deposit of faith [*ut pertinens ad fidei depositum*].[49]

The Congregation's response was "Affirmative."

> This teaching requires definitive assent, since, founded
> on the written Word of God, and from the beginning
> constantly preserved and applied in the Tradition of
> the Church, it has been set forth infallibly by the ordi-
> nary and universal Magisterium (cf. Second Vatican
> Council, Dogmatic Constitution on the Church *Lumen
> Gentium* 25, 2). Thus, in the present circumstances, the
> Roman Pontiff, exercising his proper office of confirm-
> ing the brethren (cf. Luke 22:32), has handed on this
> same teaching by a formal declaration, explicitly stat-
> ing what is to be held always, everywhere, and by all, as
> pertaining to the deposit of the faith.

The response sought to amplify the authority of Pope John
Paul II's teaching in *Ordinatio Sacerdotalis*, declaring it definitive
and infallible, but not by papal infallibility. The pope's letter was
described as a formal declaration of what bishops have always and
everywhere been definitively teaching. The Congregation thus
applied Vatican II's affirmation that bishops dispersed throughout the world can teach infallibly when, in communion with one
another, they unanimously concur that a particular teaching on a
matter of faith or morals must be held conclusively (*Lumen Gentium* 25). The Congregation concluded that Pope John Paul II's
letter *Ordinatio Sacerdotalis* had confirmed, or handed on, this
same teaching by a formal declaration, thereby making explicit
what is always and everywhere to be held by all as pertaining to
the deposit of faith. The Congregation's 1967 declaration, *Inter
Insigniores*, said that the ordination of women was "a debate which
classical theology scarcely touched upon." Would bishops always
and everywhere have seriously considered and taught something
that "classical theology scarcely touched upon" in the culture of
past centuries?

Pope John Paul II took yet one more step regarding the issue of women's ordination. On May 18, 1998, he issued an Apostolic Letter, *Ad Tuendam Fidem* (Protecting the Faith), "against errors arising from certain members of the Christian faithful, especially from among those dedicated to the various disciplines of sacred theology." It intended to prohibit further theological discussion regarding ordination of women. The Congregation for the Doctrine of the Faith simultaneously issued a new *Profession of Faith and the Oath of Fidelity on Assuming an Office to Be Exercised in the Name of the Church*.

Ad Tuendam Fidem notes that the second paragraph of the new *Profession of Faith* states, "*I also firmly accept and hold each and everything definitively proposed by the Church regarding teaching on faith and morals*," but has no corresponding canons in the Codes of the Catholic Church. The paragraph is said to be "of utmost importance since it refers to truths that are necessarily connected to divine revelation. These truths…illustrate the Divine Spirit's particular inspiration for the Church's deeper understanding of a truth concerning faith and morals, with which they are connected either for historical reasons or by a logical relationship." The lack of a canon will be remedied. Canon 750 of the Code of Canon Law will now consist of two paragraphs; the first will present the text of the existing canon; the second will contain a new text.

§ 1. Those things are to be believed by divine and catholic faith which are contained in the word of God as it has been written or handed down by tradition, that is, in the single deposit of faith entrusted to the Church, and which are at the same time proposed as divinely revealed either by the solemn Magisterium of the Church, or by its ordinary and universal Magisterium, which in fact is manifested by the common adherence of Christ's faithful under the guidance of the sacred

Magisterium. All are therefore bound to avoid any contrary doctrines.

§ 2. Furthermore, each and everything set forth definitively by the Magisterium of the Church regarding teaching on faith and morals must be firmly accepted and held; namely, those things required for the holy keeping and faithful exposition of the deposit of faith; therefore, anyone who rejects propositions which are to be held definitively sets himself against the teaching of the Catholic Church.

Canon 1371, n. 1, of the Code of Canon Law, consequently, will receive an appropriate reference to canon 750 § 2, so that it will now read:

The following are to be punished with a just penalty:

1° a person who, apart from the case mentioned in canon 1364 § 1, teaches a doctrine condemned by the Roman Pontiff, or by an Ecumenical Council, or obstinately rejects the teachings mentioned in canon 750 § 2 or in canon 752 and, when warned by the Apostolic See or by the Ordinary, does not retract;

2° a person who in any other way does not obey the lawful command or prohibition of the Apostolic See or the Ordinary or Superior and, after being warned, persists in disobedience.

Canon 598 of the *Code of Canons of the Eastern Churches* will now have two paragraphs: the first will present the text of the existing canon and the second will contain a new text. Thus canon 598, in its complete form, will read as follows:

§ 1. Those things are to be believed by divine and catholic faith which are contained in the word of God as it has been written or handed down by tradition, that is, in the single deposit of faith entrusted to the Church, and which are at the same time proposed as divinely revealed either by the solemn Magisterium of the Church, or by its ordinary and universal Magisterium, which in fact is manifested by the common adherence of Christ's faithful under the guidance of the sacred Magisterium. All Christian faithful are therefore bound to avoid any contrary doctrines.

§ 2. Furthermore, each and everything set forth definitively by the Magisterium of the Church regarding teaching on faith and morals must be firmly accepted and held; namely, those things required for the holy keeping and faithful exposition of the deposit of faith; therefore, anyone who rejects propositions which are to be held definitively sets himself against the teaching of the Catholic Church.

Canon 1436 § 2 of the *Code of Canons of the Eastern Churches*, consequently, will receive an appropriate reference to canon 598 § 2, so that it will now read:

§ 1. Whoever denies a truth which must be believed with divine and catholic faith, or who calls into doubt, or who totally repudiates the Christian faith, and does not retract after having been legitimately warned, is to be punished as a heretic or an apostate with a major excommunication; a cleric moreover can be punished with other penalties, not excluding deposition.

§ 2. In addition to these cases, whoever obstinately rejects a teaching that the Roman Pontiff or the College of Bishops, exercising the authentic Magisterium, have set forth to be held definitively, or who affirms what they have condemned as erroneous, and does not retract after having been legitimately warned, is to be punished with an appropriate penalty.

Cardinal Ratzinger supported Pope John Paul II's efforts to close further discussion of women's ordination. That is clear in the simultaneously issued "Doctrinal Commentary on the Concluding Formula of the *Professio Fidei*." Section 11 of that commentary first addressed development in the doctrine of papal infallibility. It noted that before Vatican I the discussion remained open as to whether what is understood by the primacy of papal jurisdiction and infallibility was to be considered an intrinsic part of revelation. However, that doctrine was said to be already recognized as definitive. But "only in the final stage—the definition of Vatican I—was it also accepted as a divinely revealed truth." The next paragraph then declares,

A similar process can be observed in the more recent teaching regarding the doctrine that priestly ordination is reserved only to men. The Supreme Pontiff, while not wishing to proceed to a dogmatic definition, intended to reaffirm that this doctrine is to be held definitively, since, founded on the written Word of God, constantly preserved and applied in the Tradition of the Church, it has been set forth infallibly by the ordinary and universal Magisterium. As the prior example illustrates, this does not foreclose the possibility that, in the future, the consciousness of the Church might progress to the point where this teaching could be defined as a doctrine to be believed as divinely revealed.

On October 31, 2016, Pope Francis was at Lund Cathedral in Sweden for an ecumenical commemoration of the anniversary of the Reformation ignited by Martin Luther's *Ninety-Five Theses* issued on that date in 1517. During the press conference aboard the papal plane flying back to Rome on November 2, Kristina Kappellin, from Swedish television, posed a question to Pope Francis.[50] Noting that a woman archbishop, Antje Jackelén, was head of the Swedish Lutheran Church, she asked, "What do you think: is it realistic to think of women priests also in the Catholic Church in the coming decades? And if not, why are Catholic priests afraid of competition?" The pope replied, "On the ordination of women in the Catholic Church, the final word is clear, it was said by St. John Paul II and this remains. On competition, I don't know…." Kristina Kappellin asked again, "But really forever? Never?"[51] The Pope replied, "If we read well the declaration [*Ordinatio Sacerdotalis*] made by St. John Paul II, it goes along this line, yes."

CAN ANYTHING MORE BE SAID ABOUT GOD'S WILL AND PLAN?

The "Doctrinal Commentary" presented by the Congregation for the Doctrine of the Faith makes clear that the teaching about priestly ordination being reserved only to men is not yet a doctrine to be believed as divinely revealed. It is a definitive teaching that does not presently call for the response of faith, but rather for *obedient reception*, firmly accepting and holding the papal decree. How will the teaching about priestly ordination being reserved only to men come to be seen as revealed? More crucially, how will such a teaching be received by women and men?

Admitting women to the diaconate and the priesthood will certainly involve radical changes in the patriarchal structure of the Church and its attitudes on women. Pope John Paul II declared the impossibility of ordaining women to be a definitive teaching, and forbade further discussion. But can thinking about the issue really be prohibited? Is prohibition really beneficial?

Karl Rahner ended his discussion of the Congregation for the Doctrine of the Faith's declaration, *Inter Insigniores*, by emphasizing, "Discussion Must Continue." He listed specific questions:

about the sociological emancipation of women in society and in the Church; and "about the authentic and integral essential image of the priest, which cannot be restricted to his purely sacramental power;" and about "the present-day requirements for the structure of a Christian congregation and about the function of women in the Church as determined by that structure." That involves measures to overcome discrimination against women in the Church, and finding ways of educating and changing the consciousness of the Church as a whole. Rahner further observed that we have no clear answer "of how to distinguish in principle between a 'divine' tradition and a long-enduring 'human' tradition." Theology is itself always historically conditioned, and dependent on cultural and sociological preconceptions.[52]

Similarly responding to *Inter Insigniores*, that the reservation of priestly ordination to men corresponds to "God's plan for his Church," Avery (later Cardinal) Dulles declared, "It is important for the universal Church not to let itself become bound, even unconsciously, to the sociocultural conditions of a dying age." Recognizing that "the concepts of continuity and mutability are commonly seen as incompatible," he proposed that "the opposite should be said. The Church's abiding essence actually requires adaptive change." Dulles advocated "creative innovation as a form of authentic obedience."[53]

It seems incongruous that the Church should absolutely forbid women's leadership *in persona ecclesiae* at the very time that women are more and more assuming their rightful place in human society. In 1920, women finally got the right to vote in the United States. In a 1959 referendum, three years before the Second Vatican Council, women's suffrage was rejected by 66.9% of Switzerland's men. Swiss women were finally given the right to vote, approved by 65.7% of men, in 1971, five years before *Inter Insigniores*.[54] Women have now been elected as presidents and prime ministers of countries. Is God patiently waiting for male clerics to evolve in their views of women?

The Doctrinal Commentary issued with the Profession of Faith, and signed by then-Cardinal Ratzinger, "does not foreclose the possibility that, in the future, the consciousness of the Church might progress to the point where this teaching ['that priestly ordination is reserved only to men'] could be defined as a doctrine to be believed as divinely revealed." How does that square with the theological thinking of the younger Joseph Ratzinger, who declared that if God, who

> upholds and encompasses everything, is consciousness, freedom, and love, then it follows automatically that the supreme factor in the world is not cosmic necessity but freedom...this leads to the conclusion that freedom is evidently the necessary structure of the world, as it were, and this again means that one can only comprehend the world as incomprehensible, that it must be incomprehensibility. For if the supreme point in the world's design is a freedom that upholds, wills, knows, and loves the whole world as freedom, then this means that together with freedom the incalculability implicit in it is an essential part of the world. Incalculability is an implication of freedom; the world can never—if this is the position—be completely reduced to mathematical logic.[55]

Has the Creator of such freedom and incalculability absolutely willed that women are always to be excluded as leaders in the Church?

Jesus was God become fully human. As the hymn preserved in Paul's Epistle to the Philippians (2:6–8) tells us, that entailed a self-emptying (*ekenōsen*) and vulnerability. The Council of Chalcedon in 451 declared that two natures, divine and human, were united in Jesus. He was fully divine and fully human. The two natures were not to be divided or separated, but they were likewise

97

not to be confused. "The union of natures does not annul the distinction." As the Second Vatican Council proclaimed, citing Chalcedon and the Third Council of Constantinople, Jesus "thought with a human mind" and "acted with a human will" (*Gaudium et Spes* [Constitution on Church in the Modern World] 22). He died hanging on a cross, defenseless, with never-ceasing love for God and humans.

Pope John Paul II spoke of Jesus as "giving the Church her fundamental constitution" in a way that seemed to presuppose that Jesus thought with a divine mind and decided with a divine will. The pope and the Congregation for the Doctrine of the Faith, in *Inter Insigniores*, specifically focused on Jesus calling the Twelve. They did not acknowledge that the New Testament provides no evidence that Jesus configured the leadership patterns that emerged in the postresurrection assemblies, which developed into the tripartite pattern of bishop, presbyters, and deacons.

Thomas Aquinas had maintained that Jesus had three kinds of knowledge. First, Jesus was said to have beatific vision, since his humanity already had to enjoy the vision of God that he enabled the blessed to attain after death. Second, he was said to have infused knowledge, meaning that the Logos or Word had already instilled all the intellectual concepts that Jesus's so-called possible intellect had the potential to know. Third, Jesus also had acquired or empirical knowledge whereby he grew in understanding, because his so-called agent intellect was continually transforming the experiential data coming through his senses into intellectual data.[56] Because of his beatific vision and infused knowledge, Aquinas said Jesus knew all things in the Word: "whatsoever is, will be, or was done, said, or thought, by whomsoever and at any time."[57]

In our time, to hold that Jesus did not know the future is not to deny his divinity but to reaffirm one's faith in the fullness of the incarnation. As Vatican II declared, Jesus thought with a human mind and freely decided with a human will. The International Theological Commission's 1985 document, "The Consciousness of Christ concerning Himself and His Mission," discussed the "difficult question of Christ's knowledge and consciousness."[58] As Raymond Moloney noted, the Commission made no reference to beatific vision.[59] In contemporary Catholic theology, Jesus's experience of God is understood not as some extrinsic relationship. It is integrated within his created spiritual nature and has a historical development.[60] Jesus's consciousness of sonship, his experience of closeness to God as *Abba*, was the source of all that he did and said.

Jesus came to change the culture of the world in a way that depended on human freedom. In his fully human existence, he did not exercise omnipotent power or control. His proclamation of God's reign invited hearers to live his way of service, community or *koinōnia*, and love. Reception of his invitation was dependent on a response that was freely given or refused. As noted above, he gathered a community of disciples that included unexpected persons, sinners, and outcasts. He called the Twelve, among whom Simon the Rock had a primary role. But Jesus did not establish the Church as an institution, nor leave a blueprint for that development. He did not found the Church in the manner of an architect providing a detailed drawing of every element. That is, Jesus did not bring a society into being in a way that involved both a conscious and clear idea of its constitution.[61] Rahner instead affirmed a "community" coming from Jesus, and making present Jesus, in whose life, death, and resurrection we are called to share. There always has to be a community of believers proclaiming that Jesus is not dead but alive, and that he is present in his risen life through the community sustaining its proclamation of him.[62]

The Vatican Congregation declared that Jesus's decision not to choose women as members of the Twelve was independent from and in no way responsive to the cultural norms of his lifetime. Was Jesus absolutely unresponsive and unaffected by the culture of his time, or was that portrayal of him a strategy of Vatican leadership, making their own proclamations unalterable and permanent? Would choosing women to proclaim Jesus's message have been effective in Jesus's time? Women testified to his resurrection, and their testimony was not believed *by the eleven* (Luke 24:11)!

The task given to us involves questions "that the past cannot answer for us, and the past may need us to help it answer them in fidelity to the past."[63] As John O'Malley reminds us, "We realize, perhaps to our dismay, that we cannot simply repeat the answers of the past, for the whole situation is different."[64] The salvation-historicity of the Church is still being formed by its connection with the development of concrete history.

It is remarkable that the Christian scriptures remember the names of women who accompanied Jesus during his ministry: Mary called Magdalene, Joanna the wife of Chuza who was Herod's steward, Susanna, Mary the wife of Clopas and the mother of James the younger and Joseph (Joses), and the sister of Jesus's mother, Salome, who was Zebedee's wife and the mother of James and John, "and many others" (Matt 27:56; Mark 15:40–41; Luke 8:2–3, John 19:25–26). After Jesus's death and resurrection, Mary, the mother of John Mark, Lydia, and Prisca with her husband Aquila, hosted an *ekklēsia* in their homes (Acts 12:12; 16:14–15, 40). What role would Jesus now assign to women? Would he cite the third-century text of Cyprian, and insist that women cannot represent him?

As women more and more take their place as leaders in the world, where will that leave the Church? We cannot escape from the necessity of having to deal with that future. As Rahner has noted, the future is not simply the prolongation of our past, nor merely the actualization or implementation of our present plans. It is not simply a calculated human creation involving "plans plus time." The future that comes to meet us brings surprises. "The future is that which does not evolve, that which is not planned, that which is not under our control. It is all this, and it is this precisely in its incomprehensibility and its infinitude."[65] The absolute future of humanity is the "Spirit" of God, "characterized as love and as freedom and as ever new and surprising."[66] Thus the salvation-historicity of the Church is still being formed by the Spirit guiding our response amid the development of concrete history, which allows both for continuity and the discontinuity of newness. The way forward should include a renewed eschatology that is focused on the future of the Church in this world.

7

BAPTIZED-EUCHARISTIC DISCIPLES AS AN "ORDO" STANDING WITH THE PRESIDER

THREE NOUNS, TWO in Greek and one in Latin, are associated with the "Lord's Supper" or "the breaking of bread": *anamnesis, eucharistia, missa* (remembrance, thanksgiving, mass). What the words refer to are not things but actions or activities: *remembering* Jesus's life, death, and resurrection; *giving thanks*; and *sending* (*ite missa est*)—go in peace to love and serve the Lord. As previously discussed, Cyprian claimed to be acting *vice Christi*, but in praying the eucharistic prayer, his voice was not the voice of Christ, but the voice of the assembly. Eucharistic prayers use the plural pronoun *we*, are addressed to the Father, and end by offering praise and glory to the Father, with the Holy Spirit, through, with, and in Jesus Christ.

Karl Rahner has noted that "on any realistic view of biblical theology we are not in any position to establish that in New Testament times a special power was recognized regarding the celebration of the Eucharist such that it was reserved only to a few and conferred by the laying on of hands. All that we can establish is that at the Last Supper the Lord entrusted his Church with the anamnesis [memory] of his death."[1] Baptized-eucharistic Christians, whom the Franciscan theologian Kenan Osborne identifies as the primary disciples, were the assembly (*ekklēsia*) that remembered and thanked the Father through, with, and in Jesus Christ.

The Orthodox theologian John Zizioulas notes that the Eastern churches have kept baptism and what the Western church calls confirmation inseparably linked with one another, but also with what follows, Eucharist and communion. In that regard, Zizioulas emphasizes,

> there is no such a thing as "non-ordained" persons in the Church. Baptism and especially confirmation (or chrismation) as an inseparable aspect of the mystery of Christian initiation involves a "laying on of hands" ("chrismation" in this respect is another form of the same thing)....The theological significance of this lies in the fact that *it reveals the nature of baptism and confirmation as being essentially an ordination*....the newly baptized would *take his [or her] particular "place" in the eucharistic assembly, i.e. that he [or she] would become a layman [or laywoman].* That this implies ordination is clear from the fact that the baptized person does not simply become a "Christian," as we tend to think, but he [or she] becomes a member of a particular "ordo" in the eucharistic community. Once this is forgotten, it is easy to speak of the laity as "non-ordained" and thus arrive at the possibility...of either making the layman an unnecessary element in the eucharistic community (hence the "private mass" and the entire issue of clericalism).[2]

The last sentence summarizes what happened during the medieval era, which will be considered below. Zizioulas adds, "...or of making him [the layperson] the basis of all 'orders,' as if he were not himself a specifically defined order[3] but a generic source or principle (hence the prevailing view of 'the priesthood of all believers' in all its variations)."

In his study of lay ministry in the Catholic Church, Osborne declares that third-millennium Christians will not accept statements by clerical leadership that the "lay person" has come of age, or that the post–Vatican II period of church history is a major moment for the "lay person." Osborne recalls that for centuries church leadership has not encouraged "lay persons" to be active members in the Church. "The baptized-eucharistic Christian is the primary disciple in the church." She or he should be a participant in the decision-making process of the community called Church, "and not simply as the recipient of decisions made by others."[4]

Baptized-eucharistic Christians anointed with the Spirit (chrismation) and deputized to worship were an "ordo" doing the Eucharist during the earliest centuries of the Church. As Clifford Howell makes clear, "The liturgy [Eucharist] had been regarded in early days as 'something we all do together' because that was the way it had come into being, and that was the way it was done." Gradually during the ninth and subsequent centuries, the "merely baptized" were excluded from active participation. The Eucharist "came to be regarded as 'something done by clerics and watched by the people' because that was the way it had *come* to be done….The Mass had come to look like a 'one-man sacrifice.'"[5]

In the first three centuries, baptized Christians were the *ekklēsia* (assembly) standing around a table in the home. *The General Instruction of the Roman Missal,* issued by the Congregation for Divine Worship on March 26, 1970, five years after Vatican II, directed that the faithful should stand during the Eucharistic Prayer "from the Prayer over the Gifts until the end of the Mass" except "during the silence which follows the distribution of Communion…. But, unless impeded by lack of space, density of the crowd or other reasonable cause, they should kneel down for the Consecration."[6] The Instruction added, "However, it is for the Bishops' Conference to adapt the postures and gestures here described as suitable."

The U.S. conference of bishops, supposedly to foster humility, mandated that the faithful were to kneel for the Holy, Holy,

Holy, then stand for the Our Father, and then kneel again until communion. That anomalous exception for the United States was explicitly maintained in the third edition (2010) of the *General Instruction of the Roman Missal*:

> The faithful should stand…from the invitation, *Orate, fratres* (*Pray, brethren*), before the prayer over the offerings until the end of Mass, except at the places indicated below.

> In the dioceses of the United States of America, they should kneel beginning after the singing or recitation of the *Sanctus* until after the Amen of the Eucharistic Prayer, except when prevented on occasion by reasons of health, lack of space, the large number of people present, or some other good reason. Those who do not kneel ought to make a profound bow when the priest genuflects after the consecration. The faithful kneel after the *Agnus Dei* unless the diocesan Bishop determines otherwise.[7]

In an article in the *National Catholic Reporter*, Michael Sean Winters rightly stated that it was impossible to square concern for victims with the efforts of some to weaponize the McCarrick tragedy for unrelated and incongruous objectives. Noting the outrageous smear tactics of some, and advocating mercy rather than vindictiveness, Winters defended former-Cardinal Theodore McCarrick against the charge that he had been a participant in a rebellious spirit that swept the Church after the Second Vatican Council: "There are some horror stories, to be sure, but I do not remember any of them involving McCarrick. I do remember him leading a Mass at which the congregation did not kneel during the Eucharistic Prayer. He arrested the service until everyone was on their knees."[8] Actually, that was an exercise of clerical dominion.

Kneeling emerged in the age of feudalism. In an era when serfs knelt before their earthly lords, the "nonordained" were told to kneel while the ordained stood.

A culture of hierarchical superiority survived after Vatican II in the mindsets of many bishops. The U.S. bishops imposed kneeling, a contrary sign of inferiority, on the baptized-eucharistic faithful. Their clerical culture was likewise the reason many bishops chose to protect clerical pedophiles and sexual abusers, rather than the children of the faithful. As a foundational, symbolic first step toward restoring baptized-eucharistic disciples to their initial role as an *ordo*, the faithful should once again *stand around* the altar table, along with the ordained presiders. That is how they are described (*circumstantium*) in the Latin text of the Roman Canon (Eucharistic Prayer I), whose origins precede the seventh century. When assemblies in Western European medieval churches began to kneel, those in the Eastern churches continued to stand.

MINISTRY OF THE
BAPTIZED VS. THE ORDAINED:
NOT A "DIFFERENCE OF ESSENCE"?

In 1977, Walbert Bühlmann referred to a sinister crisis in the dropping number of vocations in the Church, which he then immediately termed a salutary crisis, attributable to the Spirit re-empowering the role of the baptized in the Church.[9] External pressure led to a necessary change that involved the process of declericalization in the Church:

> The crisis in priestly vocation is the price that had to be paid if the universal priesthood of the faithful were again to be taken seriously, if the right value were to be placed on the Christian community as such. The sacred must no longer be the exclusive preserve of

priests. The whole Christian life and the whole community of the baptized is to be sacralized, in the right sense, thus releasing an unsuspected fullness of power and charisms.[10]

That perception seems borne out by developments that have given rise to a growing ministerial role for baptized persons. In 1965, The Center for Applied Research in the Apostolate (CARA) reported there were 35,925 diocesan priests in the United States and 94 percent were actively engaged in ministry; in 2021, there were 24,204 priests, and only 66 percent were active in ministry. Priests in religious orders totaled 22,707 in 1965; in 2021 they numbered 10,700. There were 898 permanent (married) deacons in 1970; in 2021 there were 18,619. In the same period, the Catholic, parish-connected population increased from 46.3 million in 1965 to 66.8 million in 2021. The precipitous drop in the number of parish priests gave rise to a growing involvement of the baptized in ministerial roles within the Church. CARA reports that, in 2015, there were 39,651 lay ecclesial ministers in parish ministry in the United States.[11]

The growth of so-called lay ecclesial ministers elicited apprehension in the Vatican. The *Instruction on Certain Questions Regarding the Collaboration of the Non-Ordained Faithful in the Sacred Ministry of the Priest*, issued on August 15, 1997, by a number of dicasteries in the Roman Curia, expressed a questionable concern for making clear the distinction between the ministries of those who are ordained and those exercised by the baptized. The document declared that the very use of the term *ministries* becomes doubtful and confused "whenever the difference of essence and not merely of degree" between the baptismal priesthood and the ordained priesthood is in any way obscured.[12]

That concern was also reflected in *Coworkers in the Vineyard of the Lord: A Resource for Guiding the Development of Lay Ecclesial Ministry*, the document issued by the U.S. Bishops' Conference in 2005.[13] It cites Pope John Paul II's 2003 exhortation on the Bishop

(*Pastores Gregis*): "The ontological and functional differentiation that sets the bishop *before* the other faithful…is a manner of *being for* the other members of the faithful; which in no way removes him from *being with* them."[14] Citing the Second Vatican Council's Constitution on the Church, the document further declares that the ordained have received a participation in the pastoral ministry that is essentially different from that given to the lay faithful.[15]

The apostle Paul's effusive praise and appreciation of his coworkers in chapter 16 of his Epistle to the Romans stands in stark contrast. Paul does not categorize his ministry as "ontologically" and "essentially" different from and superior to that of his coworkers. As Osborne has noted, "Nowhere does the New Testament indicate that the servant-leaders of the Jesus community are 'better' than the others, simply because they have been chosen to be servant-leaders."[16] Osborne contends that certain bishops and theologians who tenaciously defend an "essential" and ontological difference are fundamentally focused on the maintenance of hierarchical superiority as the fundamental criterion and priority. Gospel discipleship is never their fundamental criterion, nor is service: "The Son of Man came not to be served but to serve" (Mark 10:45).

Furthermore, "ontological difference" can hardly be applicable if there is no constant factor in the identity of a presbyter, but instead a history of variations. For example, the prayer of the bishop in the (third century?) *Apostolic Tradition*, 7, asks that the presbyter receive the Spirit of grace and counsel in order to help the bishop in overseeing the people, as the elders helped Moses in the past (Num 11:11). As discussed below, the early eighth-century *Missal of the Franks*, 33–34, introduced the ritual anointing or consecration of the hands of presbyters.[17] They were no longer primarily assistants and advisors to the bishop. Instead, their power over the Eucharist as presbyters, now called priests (*sacerdotes*), "is expressed in the anointing of [their] hands and the bestowal of chalice, bread, and wine; [their] power to forgive sins in a second imposition of hands."[18] As already noted, only in the third century did Cyprian claim the presider of the Eucharist acted *vice Christi*.

The rite for ordaining bishops came to involve an anointing of the head and the conferral of a crozier and ring, symbolizing the bishop's authority as shepherd of his church. The ritual for episcopal ordination now became coupled with the crowning of a king or emperor, which turned the bishop into a feudal lord. As bishop of Rome, Pope Leo the Great (440–61) claimed that the whole world came to Peter's See, and that the care of its bishop extended over the universal Church (*Sermon* 3.4; 4.2–3; 5.2; *Epistle* 5.2).[19] He claimed to act both as heir and *vicar* of Peter, whose faith and authority lives on in the Roman See (*Sermon* 3.2–4; *Ep.* 103). On Christmas Day in 800, Pope Leo III crowned Charlemagne, acclaimed "emperor of the Romans." Western Christendom had emerged, nurtured by an idealized vision of a universal union of all *Western* Christians in one church and state, under one pope and one Christian emperor, crowned by the pope. To overcome the problems of lay investiture, nepotism, and simony, Pope Gregory VII (1073–85) bolstered his initiatives for reform by twenty-seven principles articulated in his *Dictatus*, including: "the pope alone can use the imperial insignia" and the pope is "the only man whose feet all princes must kiss" (*Dictates* 8 and 9).[20] Calling for the First Crusade, in 1095, Pope Urban II referred to himself as "spiritual ruler of the whole world."[21] Pope Innocent III (1198–1216) did not consider it sufficient that one who could approve or depose kings and emperors should merely be "vicar of Peter." He instead maintained that, although he was successor of the Prince of the Apostles who had assumed the fullness of power,[22] he was "not the vicar of Peter or of any other apostle or human, but only of Jesus Christ himself."[23] As vicar of Jesus Christ and successor of Peter, Innocent declared himself to be "constituted as the medium between God and humans; beneath God but above humans; less than God but more than human."[24] While declaring himself "unworthy," Innocent claimed that he "held the place of God on earth" and acted as the "vicar [*vicem gerentes*]" of the "heavenly Father."[25] Napoleon's Coronation on Sunday, December 2, 1804, marked a sea change. Napoleon took the crown from the hands of Pope Pius VII and placed it on his own head. On September 20, 1870, Pope Pius IX lost his temporal power over the Papal States when he fled the Quirinale palace for the safety of the Vatican, as the army of the Italian Risorgimento took possession of Rome. The bestowal of temporal power to rule was no longer a papal prerogative.

"Every time that the meaning of 'priest' [or presbyter, or bishop] changes, the so-called 'ontological difference' also changes....What was once described as 'ontological,' 'essential,' 'metaphysical,' actually rests on what one might describe as 'existential,' 'practical,' or 'historically current' as regards the description of presbyteral or episcopal ministry." Osborne concludes that an "ontological difference" is no longer a viable theological approach for understanding the role of the baptized-eucharistic Christian in the Church, or for determining the difference between *klerikos* and *laikos*.[26]

IN THE BEGINNING:
STARTING OVER AGAIN

Eucharist, which means "giving thanks" (*eucharistein*), is an act or activity in which the entire assembly (*ekklēsia*) was originally involved. "The ordained were understood as those who presided *within* a priestly people."[27] An analysis of liturgical practice over the centuries reveals problematic *foundational* presuppositions regarding the nature of the Church, and the diminishment of the discipleship of the baptized members of the Church—evident in the complete devaluation of their role in the celebration of the Eucharist. There is a need to go back and start over.

In proclaiming the kingdom or reign of God, Jesus did not simply tell sinners and outcasts that God loved them and would be merciful to them. Jesus understood the power of symbolic action, such as breaking and sharing bread and drinking wine together at a meal. Three sources in the Gospels (Mark, Special Luke, and Q) tell us that Jesus chose to eat and drink with tax collectors and sinners (Mark 2:15–17). Being accepted unconditionally into friendship with Jesus brought a transforming change. "Now all the tax collectors and sinners were coming near to listen to him. And the Pharisees and the scribes were grumbling and saying, 'This fellow welcomes sinners and eats with them'" (Luke 15:1–2). As Gabriel Daly observed, Jesus's offer of divine forgiveness preceded moral performance on the part of those who were forgiven. "Such acceptance, was a major cause of the hostility which Jesus encountered."[28] Jesus himself summarized the negative reaction to his activity: "Look, a glutton and a drunkard, a friend of tax collectors and sinners!" (Matt 11:16–19; Luke 7:31–35).

The Last Supper stands in continuity with all the meals in which Jesus had gathered "a community of the unexpected." At the Last Supper, Jesus took bread and wine and very likely used the Aramaic word *biśrî* for body (Mark 14:22; Luke 22:19b) and the Aramaic *dĕmî* (Mark 14:24) or *bidmî* (Luke 22:20) for "my blood."[29] In the Old Testament, the Hebrew *bāśār*, "flesh," carried the connotation not only of "body" (see Ezek 11:19; 36:26; Ps 63:2; Job 4:15), but also of "person" or "self" (Num 16:22; 27:16; Isa 40:5–6; Ps 145:21).[30] In saying, "This is my body," Jesus would be identifying the bread with himself: "In giving those around the table the bread to eat, he was giving his own self."[31]

In the decades after his resurrection, the "breaking of bread" or "Lord's Supper" was a celebration in which the entire assembly (*ekklēsia*) of faithful, gathered in homes, was actively involved. In the summary in Acts 2:42–47 we are told that the followers of the risen Jesus devoted themselves to the teaching of the apostles, to fellowship (*koinōnia*), to the breaking of bread, and to prayers (Acts 2:42). They met together at the temple every day (Acts 2:46), at Solomon's Portico (5:12). They gathered in homes for "the breaking of bread," sharing their food joyfully with sincere hearts (2:44–46).

Acts also describes Paul participating in the breaking of bread at Troas. Everyone met on the first day of the week, which then began at sunset on Saturday. The assembly (*ekklēsia*) gathered in a third-floor room lit by many lamps. Intending to leave the next day, Paul kept on talking until midnight. Eutychus, who was sitting on the windowsill, was overcome by sleep and fell to the ground below. Going down, Paul took the young man in his arms and declared that he was alive. Back upstairs, Paul broke bread and ate, and continued to speak until his departure at dawn (Acts 20:7–12). Whether the passage recounts an actual assembly in which Paul participated or the kind of celebration usual when Acts was written is debated.[32] The portrayal of the assembly at Troas being attentive to an apostle's instruction and breaking bread reflects core elements in the depiction of the Jerusalem community in Acts.

In Jerusalem it was likely Greek-speaking or Hellenistic Jewish followers of Jesus who had gathered for prayer in the house of Mary, the mother of John, also called Mark (Acts 12:12). When Peter unexpectedly knocked on the outer gate at night, Mary's maid, who had the Greek name Rhoda or Rose, ran to tell everyone inside (12:13–14). After requesting that his liberation from prison be told "to James and to the believers," Peter left for another place (12:17), probably an assembly distinct from the Hellenists in Mary's house and from the Hebrews gathered around James.

Gaius, whom Paul baptized (1 Cor 1:14), was host to the whole church in Corinth (Rom 16:23). In his first letter to the Corinthians, Paul extended greetings from the church that met in Prisca and Aquila's home in Ephesus (1 Cor 16:19). Later, Paul sent greetings to the church assembled in their home back in Rome, to which they had returned, referring to the couple as working with him in Christ Jesus (Rom 16:3–5). Paul likewise greeted groups that probably assembled in two other Roman homes (Rom 16:14–15).

In Colossae, an assembly gathered in the home of the well-to-do Philemon, whose hospitality Paul himself hoped to enjoy during a visit (Phlm 22). In Philippi, the "brothers" and sisters gathered in the home of Lydia of Thyatira, a woman who was a merchant of purple cloth (Acts 16:14–15, 40). In the Epistle to the Colossians (4:15), greetings are sent to Nympha and to the church that met in her house in Laodicea.

Writing to the Corinthians, Paul speaks of the "table of the Lord" as the focal point around which the *ekklēsia* or assembly in a particular locale gathered (1 Cor 10:21; 11:18). The cup of blessing that was blessed was a *koinōnia* or communion in the blood of Christ, and the bread that was broken was a *koinōnia* or communion in the body of Christ (1 Cor 10:16). By their participation or *koinōnia* all were made into one body: "Because there is one [loaf of] bread, we who are many are one body, for we all partake of the one bread" (1 Cor 10:17). Those who were assembled were made into one body by their mutual *koinōnia* or participation in the bread and the cup become Christ's body and blood. They became what they received, the body of Christ. Although the *ekklēsia* itself is never explicitly called the body of Christ in Paul's letters, that relationship seems implied.

A DISTRIBUTION OF ROLES IN A PARTICIPATORY, PRIESTLY COMMUNITY

The New Testament does not tell us that one of the Twelve, or anyone else, presided at the Eucharist. Neither does it tell us who should preside.[33] Philippi had overseers (*episkopoi*) and deacons. Jerusalem had *presbyteroi* or elders. Acts 13:2 says that the prophets in Antioch were "engaged in liturgy [*leitourgountōn*] to the Lord," but precisely what that involved is not clear. *Didache* 10:7 says that the prophets should be allowed to give thanks, *eucharistein*, as they will. In the early decades, the emphasis was on the unique unity effected by the Eucharist, wherein all who participate become one body. We are not told who presided.

In Matthew, Luke, and John, one finds directives likely aimed at leaders of assemblies in the eighties and nineties. In Matthew, Jesus tells the Twelve, "But you are not to be called rabbi, for you have one teacher, and you are all students. And call no one your father on earth, for you have one Father—the one in heaven. Nor are you to be called instructors, for you have one instructor, the Messiah. The greatest among you will be your servant" (Matt 23:8–11). In Luke, the Twelve are portrayed arguing about which of them should be regarded as the greatest, during the Last Supper! In reaction, Jesus asks, "Who is greater: the one who is at the table or the one who serves? Is it not the one at the table? But I am among you as one who serves" (Luke 22:27). By locating the argument about precedence in the context of the Last Supper, Luke probably had in mind those claiming superiority within the assemblies of his time. That may have also been operative in the Fourth Gospel, John, written after 90. It explicitly referenced the Eucharist in chapter 6, but its version of the Last Supper does not describe Jesus saying, "This is my body, This is my blood" over bread and wine. Instead, Jesus puts on an apron, washes the disciples' feet, and directs them to do the same (John 13:4–10). He then gives a long discourse about unity and love. In the present, bishops and priests ritually wash feet only once a year, on the Thursday before Easter, but they celebrate the Eucharist every day.

The *Shepherd of Hermas*, written in Rome in installments between about 90 and 150, tells that a quest for prestige had developed among unworthy leaders and false prophets, causing tension among teachers in the church in Rome (Vision 3; Mandate 11). As a charismatic, visionary teacher, Hermas found it difficult to get the recognition connected with sitting in the teacher's section, among the front benches in the assembly. In calling all the baptized to one last repentance before the end time, Hermas included the leaders in the front seats. They were overly concerned with precedence and fomented rivalry in their ranks (Vision 2–3). Some deacons had embezzled the funds for widows and orphans (Parable 9). False prophets were vying for a seat of honor and demanding money (Mandate 11). Hermas declares that the first apostles and prophets were not guilty of such greed (Par. 9). Neither were hospitable overseers.

Only with the second century do we find an emphasis on the one who presides. Ignatius of Antioch presumed that the entire *ekklēsia* or assembly celebrates the Eucharist but insisted that a valid Eucharist is one presided by the *episkopos* or one to whom he entrusts it (*Smyrnaeans* 8). Each local assembly, united under its bishop,[34] makes present the whole, universal Church united under Christ: "Wherever the bishop appears, there the multitude of people should be, just as wherever Jesus is, there is the universal assembly [*katholikē ekklēsia*]" (*Smyrnaeans* 8:2). All the members of an undivided local church are united with their bishop, as the whole Church is with Jesus Christ (*Ephesians* 5:1). Ignatius admonishes everyone to "use" or celebrate one Eucharist, for there is one flesh of our Lord Jesus Christ, and one cup for union in his blood, one altar, just as there is one *episkopos* with the presbyters and the deacons, his fellow servants (*Philadelphians* 4:1). If the prayer of one or two is so powerful, how much more that of the bishop and the whole Church (*Eph* 5:2), who together break one bread (*Eph* 20:2).

The literature of the early centuries never spoke of the presider as "saying" the Eucharist while the congregation "heard" it. Rather, the whole community "did" the Eucharist. The bread and wine become his body and blood effected a unity of the entire community with Jesus and among themselves. All members of the assembly participated in the celebration according to their own function (*Phil.* 4; *Smyr* 8:2). Eucharist was not something "confected" by the ordained and then administered to the nonordained. It was a celebration of the entire Church. The Eucharist, presided by the bishop or by the one who represented him, was an activity in which the entire assembly of faithful was actively involved.

In the second century, Justin Martyr described the assembly for the Eucharist "on Sunday, the first day, on which God transformed darkness and matter, and created the cosmos, and on which Jesus rose from the dead" (*1 Apology* 67). The memoirs of the apostles or the writings of the prophets were read, as much as time allowed. After an exhortation "by the one presiding," the members of the assembly stood for prayers and then greeted one another with a kiss. Bread, wine, and water were presented and the one who presided *extemporaneously* offered prayers and thanksgiving *to the best of his ability*, which the people approved by saying Amen. The elements over which thanksgiving (*eucharistia*) had been offered were then shared by those present, and sent to those who were absent through the deacons. Those who had the means gave what they wished during the assembly. The one presiding used the funds to care for orphans, widows, the sick, the needy, the imprisoned, and traveling strangers staying with the community (*1 Apology* 65, 67).

As Alexandre Faivre has shown, the *kleros* or "clergy" (1 Pet 5:3) of the early Church included all believers.[35] There was a distribution of roles, not a distinction of powers, in that participatory, priestly community (1 Pet 2:9) in which Jesus was the only high priest (Heb 3:1; 4:14—5:10; 9:11; 10:21): "each Christian was active liturgically in his [or her] own way, and there was, for this reason, no real laity."[36] Christians bore witness to their faith in "nonverbal" everyday modes. Following the gospel counsels, they cared for the poor, widows, the orphaned, and the sick, and they visited prisoners.[37]

The third century will mark the beginnings of a movement away from the idea that the Christian people, with their daily life and activity, were themselves the sacrifice. That idea will gradually be displaced by an emphasis on Eucharist as sacrifice.[38] In subsequent centuries, "it will be possible to discourse extensively about the Eucharist without making reference to the Eucharistic implications for Christian living."[39] Sacrifice and Eucharist were increasingly disengaged from the previous emphasis that Christians were to live the self-giving way of Jesus in their daily lives.

Even Augustine reflected a growing stress on the Eucharist as the primary sacrifice rather than the ethical life of the faithful as the primary symbol of Christian sacrifice.[40]

ORDERS AND ORDINATION

Roman civic institutions of the third century differentiated the senatorial order (*ordo clarissimus*) and the equestrian order (of knights) from the people. *Ordinatio* was the term for appointment to such orders. Christians took over the terminology of orders. They distinguished the leadership of the Church into three orders: the order of bishops (*ordo episcoporum*), the order of presbyters (*ordo presbyterorum*), and the order of deacons. Tertullian would write: "The authority of the church constitutes the difference between the order and the people."[41]

The first text giving clear guidelines for "ordination," thereby distinguishing those who lead and serve from the rest of the community, is the *Apostolic Tradition*. A church order document, questionably attributed to Hippolytus and the third century, it provides directives for "ordination" by an imposition of hands (*cheirotonein*) into the three orders of bishops, presbyters, and deacons:

> Let him be ordained bishop who has been chosen by all the people; and when he has been named and accepted by all, let the people assemble, together with the presbytery and those bishops who are present, on the Lord's day. When all give consent, *they shall lay hands on him*, and the presbytery shall stand by and be still. And all shall keep silence, praying in their hearts for the descent of the Spirit; after which one of the bishops present, being asked by all, *shall lay his hand on him who is being ordained bishop, and pray...* (*Apostolic Tradition* 2, emphasis added).

The presbyters are ordained primarily to be advisors to the bishop in overseeing the assembly: "the bishop *shall lay his hand on his head*, the presbyters also touching him; and he shall say: 'God and Father of our Lord Jesus Christ, look upon this your servant, and impart the Spirit of grace and counsel of the presbyterate, that he may help and govern your people with a pure heart'" (*Ap. Trad.* 7, emphasis added). Only the bishop imposed hands on new deacons, since they were ordained "to the service of the bishop, to do what is ordered by him." Acting as "the hands" of the bishop in serving the needs of the community, they administer and inform the bishop regarding whatever is entrusted to them (*Ap. Trad.* 8).[42]

The *Apostolic Tradition* further instructed that widows, readers, virgins, and subdeacons are not ordained by an imposition of hands but are only instituted (*kathistasthai*) or installed (*Ap. Trad.* 10–13). That directive indicates a rising distinction between the "ordained," who lead and serve at the liturgy, and other members of the assembly.[43] Yet, the definitive clergy/laity (*klerikos/laikos*) distinction came later, about 340, in the so-called *Canons of Hippolytus*.[44] Orders are beginning their transition into "castes" in the Christian community.

In sum, from the third century onward, the clergy and the laity would be ever more segregated. Rather than a practical distribution of roles, their difference involved a distribution of powers. The clergy were considered to be in a higher *ordo* because they were devoted exclusively to the service of the altar and worked for everyone's salvation. The layman would be assigned a lower status, below that of the clergy. And the term *lay* referred primarily to men, not women.

In the early third century, the term *ekklēsia* also began to be applied not just to the assembly but to the buildings in which Christians assembled. These "church" buildings were still very modest structures, and looked like private homes, in some cases enlarged by additions. They accommodated small, intimate assemblies. As Peter Brown observes, that was the situation even in fourth-century Rome.[45] Around the year 350, "next to nothing" was recognizably Christian in Rome. It was

> almost totally empty of Christian monuments. At most, twenty-five churches lay scattered in the midst of an urban fabric made up of fourteen thousand housing blocks. What churches there were merged with the surrounding buildings. At best, they looked like modest town houses, such as were owned by the lesser nobility—a reception hall surrounded by a few subsidiary buildings entered from a courtyard. In a city of half a million, the existing churches of Rome provided room for only twenty thousand worshipers. To eyes accustomed to a traditional city, Christianity was invisible within the walls of Rome.[46]

That was not the case in the *suburbium*, the area around the city, where Constantine built spectacular Christian shrines. After his conversion in 312, Constantine erected two major basilicas: St. Peter's on the Vatican Hill and the basilica (now known as St. John Lateran) in the Lateran gardens that stretched across the hills on the southeast side of Rome.[47] The construction of vast basilica style churches, such as St. John Lateran and St. Peter's, initiated a new era of large assemblies in splendid venues. That changed the experience of the faithful, especially for women.

Christian worship "initially grew in the sphere dominated by women, that is, houses or homes. When Christianity went 'public' on a large scale in the fourth century, it entered a sphere where, in varying degrees in the larger culture, women were marginalized. A public liturgy, therefore, almost inescapably entailed some measure of marginalization for women in Christian worship."[48] Barriers emerged to set off separate areas for men and women in church buildings now described as if they were ships, hence the term *nave*. The *Apostolic Constitutions*, a late fourth-century church order document, gave instructions for how a bishop, "as one that is the commander of a great ship," should arrange the assembly, instructing the deacons as sailors to prepare places for the faithful as for passengers. The presbyters or elders were to sit on either side of the bishop's chair with the deacons standing nearby, at one end. They were said to be the sailors and officers of the ship. The people were to sit toward the other end, in complete quiet and good order; the women were to sit alone, and they likewise were to maintain silence.[49]

Married persons gradually became the "silent majority" in the Church. The historian Peter Brown has noted that most of the bishops and clerics who were the writers of the third and fourth centuries were simply not interested in thinking about the holiness of the married. "Their slogan was virginity."[50] The internal stratification of the Church and the marginalization of the "laity" especially hardened during the fourth and fifth centuries. For many bishops, "hierarchy, and not community, had become the order of the day." Ambrose of Milan, who had once been an imperial official, and Pope Siricius asserted the existence of distinct grades of perfection in the Christian life. Both believed that these distinctions could be measured in terms of the degree of a person's withdrawal from sexual activity: virgins came first, widows came second, and married persons third.[51] In Augustine's view, the Christian married couple "was to descend with a certain sadness" to the task of begetting children, for in that act their very bodies spoke to them of Adam's fall (*Sermon* 51.15,25). They were to feel a "sexual shame."[52] That is a wretched way to think about a young married couple seeking to conceive a child.

Augustine still insisted that all Christians are priests because they are members of the one priest, Christ (*City of God* 20.10), whom Augustine considered the only mediator between God and humans.[53] But the vision of the entire community of the baptized as a priestly people will fade in the face of the growing emphasis on a hierarchy of holiness. By the mid-fifth century there was a distinct

and privileged class of Christian monks and nuns, living a conti-
nent life, unencumbered by property and the weight of the social
expectations that came with wealth.[54] By the late sixth century,
when wives had more and more disappeared from the households
of the clergy and the majority of bishops came from monasteries,
the kind of clerical celibacy associated with the Western Middle
Ages had begun, a world of celibate priests, monks, and nuns.[55]
R. W. Southern has argued that medieval religious orders "were
all based on one fundamental idea—that a life fully pleasing to
God could not be lived in the secular world." The religious orders
assumed the need for a binding vow—their members' irrevocable,
lifelong commitment to penitential discipline, self-abnegation,
and prayer—"that gave religious Orders a claim to the privileges
they enjoyed." Anything less was considered a practical denial of
total dedication to God.[56] That left out the married women and
men who had once accompanied Jesus! And *fuga mundi*, or flight
from the world, is incompatible with Section 43 of the Second Vatican Council's Constitution of the Church in the Modern World,
Gaudium et Spes, which declares that Christians are bound to
fulfill earthly responsibilities: "This split between the faith which
many profess and their daily lives deserves to be counted among
the more serious errors of our age....The Christian who neglects
his temporal duties, neglects his duties toward his neighbor and
even God, and jeopardizes his eternal salvation."

Infant baptism had become the norm. A personal decision of
self-sacrificing commitment to Christ became expressed by entry
into an ascetic lifestyle, rather than by initiation into the Church
itself. It was the decision to live a celibate life that was now identified
with "conversion" or "religious" life.[57] During the sixth century,
the baptismal commitment was further devalued by Justinian's
imperial edict that all pagans report for baptismal instruction or
suffer exile and the confiscation of their property (*Codex* 1,2). This
motivation was certainly not that envisaged by 1 Peter (2:9–10)

when it described God's people as "a chosen race, a royal priesthood" called from darkness into a marvelous light.

The hierarchical developments of the fourth and fifth centuries were especially canonized by a work entitled *The Ecclesiastical Hierarchy*, written in the Eastern Church during the late fifth or early sixth centuries, under the pseudonym of Dionysius the Areopagite (Acts 17:34). In his other writings, *On Divine Names* and *The Heavenly Hierarchy*, Pseudo-Dionysius described creation as a stream of illuminating light pouring down through the uncreated Word, from a God who is Goodness, Love, boundless power, and Light. The creative cascade of light flowed down a hierarchical chain or ladder, consisting of different steps and degrees of being and understanding or "illumination" that descended from angels, through humans, to animals, plants, and rocks, the "faintest echo" of being.[58]

Presupposing hierarchy to be the order of all sacred things,[59] Pseudo-Dionysius portrayed the earthly Church as a reflection of a heavenly hierarchy, in which three triads of angels, or nine choirs, were ranked in descending order beneath the triune God. Like that heavenly hierarchy, the Church on earth was ordered into hierarchical triads.[60] Just below the angels, on the higher rungs of the ladder leading down from and back to God, is the ecclesiastical hierarchy of the "Initiators." They form a hierarchic triad that includes bishops,[61] priests, and deacons in descending order.[62] These Initiators celebrate the sacramental triad of baptismal initiation, Eucharist, and the consecration of oil, which is likewise hierarchical in the way it leads to God.[63] Below the Initiators is the triad of the "Initiated,"[64] comprising in descending order: the consecrated monks; the baptized "holy people"; and the orders of purification: penitents and catechumens. Finally, all humans are being drawn up toward the God of Light through a hierarchic triad of ascending spirituality:[65] purification or purgation of bodily desires (the beginning of growth toward perfection); contemplation or illumination (the way toward union); and finally the highest rung, union with the light that is God.

Delineating the Church in such hierarchical categories became foundational for medieval thought and practice. Thomas Aquinas thoroughly integrated the perspectives of Pseudo-Dionysius into his *Summa Theologiae*. His thinking reflected the medieval idea of *ordo*, or order. Although the Thomist tradition in still helpful today, it is not sufficient for a contemporary theological discussion of human freedom and rights. "As his attitude to slavery shows—Aquinas' idea of *ordo* was still less able to accommodate modern ideas about liberation from conditions of dependency incompatible with human dignity."[66]

DEPOSITIONING OF THE BAPTIZED: A PASSIVE AUDIENCE WATCHING THE LITURGY

The medieval period gave rise to further changes in the relationship of the faithful to the Eucharist. The growing number of Christians in the fifth century, after Theodosius declared Christianity the official religion of the empire, meant that presbyters now presided the Eucharist and began to be called priests. A movement of the altar table away from the people and further back into the apse began with the modifications that Gregory the Great made in St. Peter's basilica.[67] During the period of Romanesque architecture, the altar was pushed ever further back, so that it was close to or up against the back wall of the apse with the priest's back toward the people. Foley notes that "this architectural move of altar into the apse…was symbolic of a linguistic separation [involving Latin] that was already occurring between the baptized and presider in the central Eucharistic action."[68]

A growing multiplicity of altars within a church building fragmented the unity of the assembly and contradicted Ignatius of Antioch's directive to "use" or celebrate one Eucharist, for there is one flesh of our Lord Jesus Christ and one cup for union in his blood, one altar, just as there is one *episkopos* with the presbyters and the deacons, his fellow servants (*Phila.* 4:1). Each priest, now with his back toward the people, silently said his "low mass," since praying aloud or singing would disturb others. The Eucharist had become an action of the priest, who celebrated silently, and often privately. "Evidence of priests saying mass without a congregation may come from as early as the seventh century."[69] A great physical and spiritual distance had emerged between the priest and the people.

Given the cultural environment north of the Alps, which focused on ritual consecration of altars, patens or plates, cups (*calices*), and even churches, it would be logical that the hands of those who touched all those things, should also be anointed. Thus, the ordination rite in the eighth century *Missal of the Franks* introduced the anointing of the hands of the presbyters, now called priests.[70] The patens or plates for the eucharistic bread and the cups (*calices*) were consecrated at the very time when the faithful were restricted in the way that they could receive communion. Beginning with the seventh century, communion in the hand was prohibited for the baptized, so they could no longer take it home to the sick. In the ninth century, the eucharistic bread, now small unleavened hosts, was generally placed on the tongue.[71] Communion from the cup for the baptized disappeared by the end of the thirteenth century.[72] The nonordained were likewise no longer allowed to touch the paten or the cup, which were now to be made from gold or silver, or at least tin, for poorer churches. Foley remarks that such silver or gold vessels now replaced the baptized, who were meant to be *living vessels* of the presence of Christ.[73]

The Eucharistic Prayer in the *Apostolic Tradition*, 4, had portrayed the baptized faithful in an active, participatory role, having self-regard: "We offer you the bread and the cup, giving you thanks because you have deemed us worthy to stand before you and serve you."[74] An emphasis on humanity's sinfulness, rooted in Augustine's development of the doctrine of original sin, and a stress on the divinity of Jesus—in reaction to Arianism and Adoptionism—imbued the baptized with a sense that they were unworthy to receive the Eucharist.[75] "By the beginning of the early Middle Ages ordinary Christians considered themselves more sinful than graced, more unlike than like God, and unworthy for something as sacred as communion."[76]

Celibacy had been a freely chosen option in the first century of the Church (1 Cor 7:25–35). But celibacy and virginity had now become hallmarks of the really committed, and two strata were ever more defined within the Western Church. Those living "a more perfect holiness" were distinguished from the rest of the baptized, particularly the faithful who could procreate children. What Paul asked was forgotten: "Do we not have the right to be accompanied by a believing wife, as do the other apostles, and the brothers of the Lord and Cephas?" (1 Cor 9:5). So was the directive about choosing an overseer who nurtured his family well (1 Tim 3:4; Titus 1:6).

Canon 46 of the *Penitential of Vinnian*, from the sixth century, recommended abstinence from sexual relations for the baptized faithful during "the three forty-day periods" (before Christmas and Easter, and after Pentecost) and also on Saturday nights and Sundays.[77] In the seventh century, the *Penitential of Cummean* (2.30) added the traditional penitential days of Wednesday and Friday. The eighth century *Penitential* (or *Canons*) *of Theodore* proposed that married couples should abstain from sexual relations for three days before communion (2.12.1). Women were forbidden to enter a church or to receive communion during menstruation and for forty days after childbirth (1.14.19; cf. Lev 12:1–5). Such initiatives flowed from a deficient view of marriage and human sexuality. The primary goal of marriage was said to be the procreation and instruction of children; its secondary goals were the alleviation of concupiscence or sexual desire and mutual help. Centuries would pass before the Second Vatican Council's Constitution on the Church in the Modern World, *Gaudium et Spes* 49–50, finally spoke of mutual love as a primary goal of marriage and an attribute of sexual union in marriage.

The architectural splendor of gothic churches still enchants us, but one must remember that a hierarchical order was determined within those churches by one's proximity or distance from the altar. Rood screens that blocked a view of the altar were a barrier in many churches. Bells would be rung to signal what was happening at the altar now pushed back, more like a shelf than a table, and out of the sightline of many of the faithful. Their participation was absolutely minimized.

Osborne has noted that "western church leadership, whether monastic or episcopal, did not provide the ordinary lay Catholic with very many facets of spirituality."[78] Mostly they were told what they should not do. Church leadership was focused on the "more perfect way" of discipleship of monks and nuns. The result was what Osborne has termed a "depositioning" of the "unordained" baptized members of the Church. They were not provided with a spirituality that recognized and nurtured the "discipleship" to which they were called by Jesus. "The very term 'church' came to mean the leadership of the church, thus implying that 'true' discipleship was found primarily in celibate church leadership."[79]

In the eleventh century, Berengar of Tours denied that the bread and wine are changed to become the body and blood. For him, they remained signs. For, if they were not signs of a spiritual presence, how could they be a sacrament?[80] The controversy led to the concept of transubstantiation. The intensified emphasis on real presence generated by the controversy made believers more eager to 'see' the Eucharist.[81] Thus the seldom-received Eucharist began to be "exposed" for the adoration of the faithful, who would rush into churches when they heard the bell signaling the now heightened "moment of consecration." The elevation of the host, introduced during the twelfth and thirteenth centuries, would sometimes be prolonged for minutes.[82] The practice of genuflecting before the Eucharist (in imitation of what one did before an

earthly king or feudal lord in that era) emerged after the contro-
versies of the eleventh century and began to make its way into the
rituals of the Mass during the fourteenth century.

By the eleventh century, the priest was usually the only one
who ate and drank the Eucharist. He came out to see if anyone else
wished to receive only after removing his vestments at the end of
Mass. Instead of transforming the faithful into the body of Christ
through their communion, the seldom-received Eucharist was
transformed into the greatest of the relics so revered by medieval
Christians. Showing or exposition of a consecrated host in a mon-
strance, and blessing, or benediction, with it emerged. Chapter 21
of the Fourth Lateran Council in 1215 required reception of the
Eucharist at least once a year at Eastertime. Thomas Aquinas and
later the Council of Trent favored more frequent communion.[83]
Some theologians later characterized the communion of the faithful, who had become passive and marginalized observers at a liturgy celebrated by the ordained, as not essential for "the sacrifice
of the mass."[84]

No longer was "one bread (or loaf) broken and shared" by the
many who thereby became one body (1 Cor 10:16–17). Beginning
with the ninth century, Western churches began to use unleavened
bread (on the assumption that the Last Supper was a Passover
meal) and then, during the eleventh and twelfth centuries, introduced the preformed small wafers still prevalent today. By the thirteenth century, some Western churches likewise gave communion
only under the form of bread. "Communion from the cup by the
faithful came to an end."[85] During the fifteenth century, the Council of Constance made communion only under the form of bread
into a universal law, reacting to the arguments for communion
under both kinds made by John Wycliff (c. 1330–84) and Jan Hus
(c. 1370–1415).[86] Their positions regarding the doctrine of transubstantiation, and indulgences, would likewise be condemned
as heretical at the Council of Constance in 1415, where Hus was
burned alive at the stake.

Just over a hundred years later, on October 31, 1517, Martin Luther precipitated the Protestant Reformation with his *Ninety-Five Theses* calling for public disputation on indulgences.[87] Luther's *Letter to the Christian Nobility of the German Nation*, written in August 1520, declared that "all Christians are truly of the spiritual estate, and there is no difference among them except that of office....We are all one body, yet every member has its own work by which it serves the others." Baptism, gospel, and faith alone make us spiritual, and a Christian people. "We are all consecrated priests through baptism, as St. Peter says in 1 Peter 2[:9], 'You are a royal priesthood and a priestly realm.' The Apocalypse says, 'Thou hast made us to be priests and kings by thy blood' [Rev 5:9–10]."[88] In Luther's mind, when a bishop consecrates one who says Mass, or preaches, or gives absolution, "it is nothing else than that in the place and stead of the whole community, all of whom have like power, he takes a person and charges him to exercise this power on behalf of the others."[89] In his *Babylonian Captivity of the Church*, published two months later, Luther again emphasized the priesthood of the baptized. Invoking 1 Peter 2:9, he proclaimed, "We are all priests, as many of us as are Christians. But the priests, as we call them, are ministers chosen from among us. All that they do is done in our name; the priesthood is nothing but a ministry."[90] Complaining that the world is filled with priests, bishops, and cardinals who repetitiously mumble prayers as hour-readers and Mass-sayers but do not preach, he concluded that "whoever does not preach the Word, though he was called by the church to do this very thing, is no priest at all, and that the sacrament of ordination can be nothing else than a certain rite by which the church chooses its preachers."[91] According to Luther, "It is the ministry of the Word that makes the priest and the bishop," not blessing churches and bells, or confirming children.[92] Luther proclaimed all Christians to be priests through their baptism, but he did not consider all to be pastors. The role of "pastor" in the Church requires that "an office and a field of work" be committed to one's charge: "This call and command make pastors and preachers."[93]

FROM THE REFORMATION TO VATICAN II: RIGIDITY AND RUBRICISM

The baroque architecture of the Jesuit Church of the *Gesù* in Rome, built between 1568 and 1575, sought to bring the congregation closer to the liturgical action. The apse was shortened and the choir area, or chancel, in front of the altar was eliminated, to bring the altar closer to the congregation. (Rood screens were no longer installed and had been removed in older churches.) In this new design, churches began to resemble a theater. A raised sanctuary, shortened apse, and elimination of visible barriers including lack of interior columns turned the high altar into a virtual stage. Tabernacles attached to the main altar became an architectural feature.[94] As Edward Foley notes, "Like an audience, the assembly could now watch the drama of the mass unfold before them with few visible obstructions....The actors in the liturgy, however, did not include the assembly, but only the ministers in the sanctuary, particularly the priest. Thus, while the assembly was physically closer to the Mass celebrated in such a building, they remained liturgically distant."[95] Baroque architecture allowed for more people to participate. But participation was understood as a visual experience, rather than an action done by all of those assembled. Participation was watching the ritual.

Before the invention of the movable-type printing press, liturgical books had been handmade manuscripts, with immense variations reflecting the locales in which they were produced. There was no oversight from a central authority. In responding to the criticisms and innovations of the Protestant Reformers, the Church likewise sought to correct abuses involving liturgical practice. The commission that produced the Missal of Pius V in 1570 was responding to the chaotic situation that existed in liturgical books at the time. The remedy was the imposition of uniformity, achieved by the printing of a reformed Missal.

Unfortunately, a genuine understanding of liturgy as a celebration that involved all the members of the Church was far from the mind of the Council of Trent, Pope Pius V, or the commission that produced the Missal. In 1570, there was no impulse for reinstating an active liturgical role for the baptized. Zeal for emphasizing the ministerial priesthood, over against Luther's emphasis on the priesthood of the baptized, caused the latter idea to fade from the consciousness of the baptized. A reform that would elicit active participation was not even envisaged: the priest remains the sole actor in a "one-man sacrifice." It is something he does all by himself, rather than "something we all do together, as it was in early days."[96] The reform did nothing to eliminate exclusion of the laity or unintelligibility (Latin).

From 1570 onward, a rigid uniformity prevailed.[97] "Nothing in the liturgy itself could be changed or developed. Every word printed in black had to be uttered, every action printed in red had to be performed....A special branch of knowledge was developed for this purpose—the science of rubrics [from the Latin word for *red*]." In the three lengthy documents that introduced Pius V's Missal, *Rubricae Generales*, *Ritus Servandus*, and *De Defectibus*, there are many minute details about what a celebrating priest must do, but only two incidental mentions of the people.[98]

Toward the end of the seventeenth century, the discovery of some early liturgical documents revealed that in early centuries the liturgy was a genuinely communal celebration. But attempts to restore active participation in France and Germany were suppressed by authorities, partly because "whatever was not prescribed by rubrics was forbidden....A few prayerbooks containing translations of the Mass prayers were published; they, too, were condemned."[99] Abbot Prosper Guéranger (1805–75) of the monastery of Solesmes fostered a more monastic study of the liturgy, including its history and theology. In his *Institutions Liturgiques*, he cited Pope Alexander VII's rebuke, in 1661, of those who "boldly translated the Roman Missal into French, previously printed in Latin, in accord with the established and approved custom of the Church....They degraded the sacred rites by taking away the majesty which the Latin language provided, and by exposing the sacred mysteries to all eyes."[100] Guéranger did not disagree. He would never translate the Canon of the Mass. In opposition to the Protestant Reformers who said the people should be able to understand, Guéranger maintained that Latin was essential for keeping the Canon in a language mysterious to the people. It enabled a concealment that he favored.[101] That did not presage future developments. Vernacular Missals were dropped from the Index of Forbidden Books in 1897. Given the limits of enforcing such a law, some had earlier eluded being suppressed.

Pope Pius X published his *motu proprio* on Sacred Music, *Tra le Sollecitudini*, on November 22, 1903. He declared, "Efforts must be made to restore the use of the Gregorian chant by the people, so that the faithful may again take a more active part in the ecclesiastical offices, as they were wont to do in ancient times."[102] Two years later, the decree *Sacra Tridentina Synodus* advocated that the faithful receive communion at each Mass they attend.[103] James White considers that to be "the most important reform in Roman Catholic worship in centuries, gradually leading to an ever increasing number of laity receiving Communion every week."[104]

Dom Lambert Beauduin (1873–1960) of the abbey of Mont-César in Louvain, Belgium, expounded on Pius X's concept of active participation in a paper at the Congress of Malines in 1909. The resolutions passed by that congress were the same as those with which Beauduin ended his paper: to spread the use of the Missal as a book of piety and to make piety more liturgical.[105] In a later book, *La piété de l'église* (1914), Beauduin developed a theology of active participation based on the priesthood of Christ, the Church as his mystical body, and the shared priesthood of all the baptized.[106] Remarkably, while strongly advocating for the vernacular Missal, Beauduin remained opposed to the vernacular Mass. "He apparently considered it sufficient for people to know what the priest was saying."[107]

PIUS XII AND THE PERSPECTIVES OF *MEDIATOR DEI*

Pope Pius XII's encyclical *Mediator Dei* (On the Sacred Liturgy), issued in 1947, offered a guarded nod to the then-growing liturgical movement.[108] Accepting that the liturgy of the Church as a living organism "grows, matures, develops, adapts and accommodates to temporal needs and circumstances," the encyclical nonetheless decried "the temerity and daring" of novel innovations such as making use of the vernacular in the celebration of the "august" eucharistic sacrifice (59). It declared that the use of the Latin language, customary in a considerable portion of the Church, is a manifest and beautiful sign of unity, as well as an effective antidote (as a dead language) for any corruption of doctrinal truth. It granted that the use of the vernacular in several of the rites may be of much advantage to the people, but insisted that the Apostolic See alone is empowered to grant this permission (60).

Mediator Dei declared that "one would be straying from the straight path were he to wish the altar restored to its primitive tableform; were [one] to want black excluded as a color for the liturgical vestments"(62). The encyclical noted that some disapproved of Masses offered privately and without any congregation, on the ground that they are a departure from the ancient way of offering the sacrifice. Some were also saying that priests should not offer Mass at different altars at the same time, because, by doing so, they separated the community of the faithful and imperiled its unity. Pius declared those who advocated such positions were "mistaken in appealing to the social character of the eucharistic sacrifice, for as often as a priest repeats what the divine Redeemer did at the Last Supper, the sacrifice is really completed" (95, 96).

In that regard, the encyclical likewise repeatedly asserted that the integrity of the eucharistic sacrifice only requires that the priest receive communion. That the people should also receive communion was said to be desirable, but it was not required for the integrity of the sacrifice (112). Pius maintained that the eucharistic sacrifice of its very nature is the unbloody immolation of the divine Victim, made manifest in a mystical manner by the separation of the sacred species and by their oblation to the eternal Father. Communion pertains to the integrity of the Mass and to the partaking of the august sacrament; but while it is obligatory for the priest who says the Mass, it is only something earnestly recommended to the faithful (115).

The encyclical further declared that the then-emerging "dialogue" Mass "cannot replace the high Mass, *which, though it be offered with only the sacred ministers present* [emphasis added], possesses its own special dignity due to the impressive character of its ritual and the magnificence of its ceremonies." It granted that the splendor and grandeur of a high Mass are very much increased if, as the Church desires, the people are present in great numbers and with devotion (106). But the encyclical again insisted that the integrity of the Mass as an unbloody sacrifice requires only the priestly action of the ordained; *the people's participation, referred to as a public or social dimension, is deemed desirable but unnecessary for the integrity of the sacrifice.* For Pius XII, the faithful remain passive participants, watching a sacrifice being offered by the priest. Only the actions of the priest were deemed *necessary.* Pius was utterly imbued in medieval developments, and he rejected most of the liturgical reforms that would be implemented after Vatican II.

Mediator Dei said that "the faithful should be aware that to participate in the eucharistic sacrifice is their chief duty and supreme dignity, and that not in an inert and negligent fashion, giving way to distractions and day-dreaming, but with such earnestness and concentration that they may be united as closely as possible with the High Priest" (80). He added, "The fact, however, that the faithful participate in the eucharistic sacrifice does not mean that they also are endowed with priestly power" (82). Pius insists it is very necessary that bishops make this quite clear to their flocks (81).

The specter of Martin Luther remains: the encyclical strongly opposes "those who...teach that in the New Testament by the word 'priesthood' is meant only that priesthood which applies to all who have been baptized; and hold that the command by which Christ gave power to His apostles at the Last Supper to do what He Himself had done, applies directly to the entire Christian Church, and that thence, and thence only, arises the hierarchical priesthood" (83). Asserting " that the people are possessed of a true priestly power, while the priest only acts in virtue of an office committed to him by the community, they look on the eucharistic sacrifice as a "concelebration," in the literal meaning of that term, and consider it more fitting that priests should "concelebrate" with the people present than "that they should offer the sacrifice privately when the people are absent." Pius emphasizes that "the priest acts for the people only because he represents Jesus Christ, who is Head of all His members and offers Himself in their stead (84). Hence, he goes to the altar as the minister of Christ, *inferior to Christ but superior to the people* [emphasis added]. Since the people in no sense represent the divine Redeemer and are not mediator between themselves and God, they can in no way possess the sacerdotal power." Pius's defense of priestly power over the Eucharist does not see the need to recognize a fuller and more active participation for the baptized-eucharistic faithful. Article 108 of the encyclical shows Pius's narrow assessment of the faithful:

> Many of the faithful are unable to use the Roman missal even though it is written in the vernacular; nor are all capable of understanding correctly the liturgical rites and formulas. So varied and diverse are men's talents and characters that it is impossible for all to be moved and attracted to the same extent by community prayers,

hymns and liturgical services. Moreover, the needs and inclinations of all are not the same, nor are they always constant in the same individual. Who, then, would say, on account of such a prejudice, that all these Christians cannot participate in the Mass nor share its fruits? On the contrary, they can adopt some other method which proves easier for certain people; for instance, they can lovingly meditate on the mysteries of Jesus Christ or perform other exercises of piety or recite prayers which, though they differ from the sacred rites, are still essentially in harmony with them.

In section 82 of his earlier encyclical *Mystici Corporis Christi*, issued in 1943, Pius refers to the Eucharist: "In this Sacrifice the sacred minister acts as the viceregent not only of our Savior but of the whole Mystical Body and of each one of the faithful. In this act of Sacrifice through the hands of the priest, by whose word alone the Immaculate Lamb is present on the altar, the faithful themselves, united with him in prayer and desire, offer to the Eternal Father a most acceptable victim of praise and propitiation for the needs of the whole Church." Pius's presuppositions reflect the historical process in which the baptized gradually moved from an active to a passive role. He showed little concern for restoring the baptized-eucharistic disciples of Christ to the fuller role that they had once enjoyed.

VATICAN II: A GOAL OF FULL AND ACTIVE PARTICIPATION

In its return to the sources, the Constitution on the Liturgy, *Sacrosanctum Concilium*, sought to retrieve the early centuries' vision of Church as a particular or local community assembled for the Eucharist. Article 2 of the Constitution emphasizes that "it is through the liturgy, especially, that the faithful are enabled to express in their lives and manifest to others the mystery of Christ and the real nature of the true Church." That statement prevailed despite opposition by a minority clinging to the ecclesiology of the eighteenth and nineteenth centuries, which primarily identified the essence of the Church with its juridical organization as a "perfect society," as exemplified in Pius XII's encyclical.[109]

Section 14 declares, "Mother Church earnestly desires that all the faithful should be led to that fully conscious, and active participation in liturgical celebrations which is demanded by the very nature of the liturgy. Such participation by the Christian people as 'a chosen race, a royal priesthood, a holy nation, a redeemed people (1 Pet. 2:9; cf. 2:4–5), is their right and duty by reason of their baptism.'"

> In the restoration and promotion of the sacred liturgy, this full and active participation by all the people is the aim to be considered before all else; for it is the primary and indispensable source from which the faithful are to derive the true Christian spirit; and therefore pastors of souls must zealously strive to achieve it, by means of the necessary instruction, in all their pastoral work. Yet it would be futile to entertain any hopes of realizing this unless the pastors themselves, in the first place, become thoroughly imbued with the spirit and power of the liturgy, and undertake to give instruction about it. A prime need, therefore, is that attention be directed, first of all, to the liturgical instruction of the clergy.

Under the heading "Norms Drawn from the Hierarchic and Communal Nature of the Liturgy," section 26 begins by saying that "liturgical services are not private functions, but are celebrations of the Church, which is 'the sacrament of unity,' namely, the holy people united and organized under their bishops."[110] Liturgical services "touch individual members of the Church is different ways, depending on their orders, their role in the liturgical services, and their actual participation in them." The Constitution emphasizes that "rites that are meant to be celebrated in common, with the faithful present and actively participating, should as far as possible be celebrated in that way rather than by an individual and quasi-privately."

Referring to the Epistles of Ignatius of Antioch, article 41 emphasizes that "the principal manifestation of the Church consists in the full active participation of all God's holy people in the same liturgical celebrations, especially in the same Eucharist, in one prayer, at one altar, at which the bishop presides, surrounded by his college of priests and by his ministers." Article 42 declares that communal liturgical celebrations in parishes, "under a pastor who takes the place of the bishop, are the most important, for in some way they represent the visible Church constituted throughout the world." The Constitution on the Liturgy recovered a long lost but foundational doctrine—that the full and active participation of the baptized is essential to the liturgical celebration of the Eucharist. It thereby initiated Vatican II's retrieval of the concept of the particular or local church, which understands that the universal Church is actualized in and through the community of a particular locale, most especially when it assembles in prayer, thanking God for sharing and transforming our humanity in Jesus and for sending the Spirit into our midst. That foundational role of the Eucharist would be reiterated throughout the Constitution on the Church, particularly in articles 3, 7, 10, 11, and 26.

In treating the Church as a "visible structure," *Lumen Gentium* deliberately moves beyond the perspectives of Robert Bellarmine, who compared the visibility of the Church to the unity of the kingdom of France or the Republic of Venice.[111] Unlike Pius XII's encyclical *Mystici Corporis Christi*, the constitution does not simply identify "the society structured with hierarchical organs" with "the mystical body of Christ," or "the visible society" with "the spiritual community," or "the earthly Church" with "the

Church endowed with heavenly riches." While emphasizing that the elements of each pair do *not* represent "two realities," article 8 describes them as "one complex reality which comes together from a human and a divine element," analogously invoking the incarnation uniting the human *and* divine.

Chapter 2 of *Lumen Gentium* declares that God makes humans holy and saves them not just as individuals without any mutual connection, but by making them into a people, like the Jewish people. In that regard, the Church as the people of God (1 Pet 2:9–10) is a historical community of humans living in time and place, but always simultaneously permeated by an essential universality. As "the visible sacrament of this saving unity…while it transcends all limits of time and confines of race, the Church [as the people of God] is destined to extend to all regions of the earth and so enters into the history of mankind" (*Lumen Gentium* 9).

Article 10 describes the people of God as a priestly people, meaning that all the baptized and the ordained together share a "common priesthood of the faithful" in which all have equal dignity. That common priesthood of all who form the Church is said to be essentially different from "the ministerial or hierarchical priesthood," although there was much discussion within the Council about the ways in which the "priesthood of the faithful" and the "ministerial priesthood" are dissimilar and similar.[112] The final text describes ministerial priests as endowed with a sacred power by which they "form and rule" the priestly people, but at the same time emphasizes that the common priesthood of the faithful and the ministerial priesthood are mutually ordered to one another. Both participate, in distinctive modes, in the one priesthood of Christ. The "priestly community" of all the faithful is said to be actualized both in the celebration of the sacraments and in virtuous living. The unity of God's priestly people, deputized to worship by the baptismal character, is most aptly signified and effected by their celebration and reception of the Eucharist (*Lumen Gentium* 11).

FULL AND ACTIVE PARTICIPATION: AN UNACHIEVED GOAL

Vatican II renewed about 20 percent of ecclesial culture. In the postconciliar implementation of liturgical "renewal," the Eucharist was celebrated in the vernacular, altars again became tables at which the presider faced the assembly, and, in most churches, the rail that had separated the faithful from the so-called sanctuary was removed. During a Sunday celebration of the Eucharist at the main altar of a church, there was to be no other celebration at a side altar, since this practice would divide the oneness of the assembly or church. Such changes were a creative retrieval of the eucharistic assemblies of the earliest centuries, and clearly moved beyond the boundaries that *Mediator Dei* sought to impose.

Communion in the hand is now common, as it was in the early centuries, although it was not initially approved in the United States because some bishops thought that having the baptized touch the Eucharist would diminish the distinction between the priest and the people. The presider at the altar table still likely thinks of himself as representing Jesus. "Full and active participation" has not come to mean that the liturgy is once again regarded as "something we all do together." The laity do not think of themselves as doing the Eucharist. Architectural changes, such as rearranging the liturgical space and moving the altar table, are not sufficient to empower the full participation of the entire community. The celebration of the Eucharist is still "something done by clerics and watched by the people." The priests stand; in the United States, the faithful kneel. They remain a lower caste below clerics.

Vatican II never achieved "full and active participation of all God's holy people" because it never sought to reestablish equality in discipleship. It juxtaposed a commitment to full and active participation by the baptized with a continued emphasis on hierarchy. There must be more attention to nurturing a spirituality of "discipleship" for all the baptized. Greater effort must be given to instruction concerning the priesthood of the faithful. In that regard, assemblies should be invited to consider the fact that "the one who presides" always prays the Eucharistic Prayer in the first-person plural, "we." The baptized-eucharistic faithful are an *ordo* deputized to celebrate the Eucharist as an action they all do together with the ordained presider. A full and active participation in which all the baptized are told to kneel, while a group of ordained presiders/concelebrants remains standing around the altar table bespeaks hierarchical differentiation rather than a distribution of roles in a participatory, priestly community.

In his opening address to the 2018 Synod of Bishops on Young People, Pope Francis declared, "Clericalism arises from an elitist and exclusivist vision of vocation that interprets the ministry received as a *power* to be exercised rather than as a free and generous *service* to be given. This leads us to believe that we belong to a group that has all the answers and no longer needs to listen or learn anything, or that pretends to listen."[113] As Pope Francis suggests, it is high time to shake free of Catholic clericalism. Reestablishing the essential, foundational role of the baptized faithful standing as an "ordo" alongside those ordained as bishops and presbyters would overturn the passive role imposed on the baptized over the course of centuries.

Vatican II's Constitution on the Church (section 10) describes the people of God as a priestly people, meaning that all the baptized and the ordained together share a "common priesthood of the faithful" in which all have equal dignity (1 Pet 2:9). The faithful must discard the inferior role assigned to them over the centuries and again stand with the ordained presiders before the altar table. That will mark a first, decisive step toward regaining their rightful role and voice as an *ordo* in the Church. The Eucharist must again come to be understood as "something we all do together," *each in their own role*. There is need to ignite such change. Statistics from the Center for Applied Research in the Apostolate (CARA) at Georgetown University, report that in 1970 weekly Mass attendance was 54.9 percent (monthly 71.4 percent); in 2018–19 weekly was 21.1 percent (monthly 45.3 percent); in 2021 weekly was 17.3 percent (monthly 36.6 percent). A downward, or upward, spiral is evident in other crucial statistics. In 1970 there were 426,309 marriages in Catholic churches in the United States; in 2017 there were 143,082; in 2018 137,885; in 2019, 131,827; in 2020 *amid the COVID-19 epidemic*, 97,200. In 1970 there were 3.5 million former Catholic adults in the United States; in 2018 there were 26.1 million; in 2019–20 there were 29 million; in 2021 there were 39.6 million. In 1970, 45.8 percent of Catholics said their affiliation was "strong;" in 2018–19 the number was 32.2 percent.[114] There is a need to emphasize the ecclesial role of baptized members within the Church. They are the *ekklēsia* and are not to be taken for granted by the ordained claiming an ontological or essential superiority.

Making clear that celebration of the Eucharist is really "something we all do together," bishops and priests in the United States should invite their assemblies to stand once again with them, *circumstantes* around the altar table. That would *begin* to break the shell of clericalism and implant a new mindset. The celebration that transforms bread and wine into the body and blood of Christ has always had a more ultimate goal: the transformation of the entire assembly or *ekklēsia* into the body of Christ. In the words of Paul's First Epistle to the Corinthians, "We who are many are one body, for we all partake of the one bread" (10:17). In Sermon 272 on the Eucharist, preached on Pentecost Sunday, Augustine recalled Paul's words: "You are the body of Christ and individually members of it" (1 Cor 12:27). He then added, "It is your mystery [the sacramental *symbol* of yourselves] which is placed on the Lord's table. It is your mystery you receive....You hear the words 'the body of Christ' and you answer 'Amen.' Be a member of Christ." The faithful are not presiders but they are a priestly people. *They are the ekklēsia*, the assembly that *is members of the body of Christ*. The Eucharist is not a one-man sacrifice; it is an act that involves the entire priestly people.

8

EPILOGUE

Love is the most decisive decision made possible by freedom. We decide ourselves who and what we want to be and our relationship with others and with God. In Romans 12—13 and in 1 Corinthians 12—13, Paul presents love as the most important gift of the Spirit. His list of "the works of the flesh" in Galatians (5:19–21; see also 5:13–15) are in great part concerned with problems in community or interpersonal relationships. By contrast, the fruit of the Spirit is: love, joy, peace, patience, kindness, goodness, faithfulness, gentleness, and self-control (Gal 5:22–23).

The synoptics all place love of neighbor on a par with love of God (Mark 12:28–34; Matt 22:34–40; Luke 10:25–28; cf. Deut 6:5; Lev 19:18). The judgment scene in Matthew 25:31–40 provides instruction about the way in which the followers of Jesus should act in the present.[1] The Son of Man welcomes into the kingdom prepared "from the foundation of the world" those who gave food to the hungry, drink to the thirsty, a welcome to strangers, clothing to the naked, and who cared for the sick and visited the imprisoned. It presumes Jesus is related with all humans. The Epistle of James in its emphasis on good works harmonizes with Matthew 25. The epistle denounces the suffering of the poor at the hands of the rich: "Has not God chosen the poor in the world to be rich in faith and to be heirs of the kingdom that he has promised to those who love him?" (2:5).

Matthew 25 and James remind us that we live our faith by caring for our brothers and sisters. "Loving one another" as Jesus has loved us is the core of the discourse in John 15:9–17. The First Epistle of John likewise makes love primary: "Whoever does not love does not know God, for God is love.…We love because [God] first loved us. Those who say, 'I love God,' and hate their brothers or sisters are liars; for those who do not love a brother or sister whom they have seen, cannot love God whom they have not seen.…Those who love God must love their brothers and sisters also" (1 John 4:8, 19–21).

Acts of the Apostles refers to the followers of Jesus living "the Way," of the Lord or of God.[2] In his way of being human, Jesus redefined God and humanity. Edward Schillebeeckx emphasizes that Jesus was opposed to the idea of a triumphant messiah:

> Like God, Jesus identifies himself *par excellence* with outcast and rejected men and women, the unholy, so that he too himself finally becomes the one who is rejected and outcast.…Jesus is not condemned because as a man he is said to have divine pretensions, nor for his weak humanity.…He is condemned for his sovereign and free human way of life, which is subversive to any one who gambles and bets on power.…His behavior compelled the powerful to unmask themselves. He criticizes the perverse effects of a particular zeal for "God's cause" to the detriment of the "human cause."…Jesus refuses to heal human violence in our history through "divine force."…Jesus' death on the cross is the consequence of a life in radical service of justice and love, a consequence of his option for the poor and the outcast, of a choice for his people suffering under exploitation and oppression.[3]

"Although God always comes in power, divine power knows no use of force. Not even against people who are crucifying his

Christ."[4] That has not been true of the hierarchical Church. Giordano Bruno was named Filippo at his baptism and later called "Il Nolano" because of his birth in Nola, near Naples, in 1548. When he became a Dominican friar, he took the name Giordano and was ordained a priest in 1572. Accused of heresy for discussing Arianism, he fled Naples for Rome, and then Geneva, Toulouse, Paris, London, and Oxford. In February 1584, he gave a series of lectures in Oxford about the Copernican theory and the movement of earth around the sun, which resulted in a hostile reaction. He began to write his "Italian Dialogues," of which three were cosmological. Maintaining a sun-centered world, he proposed an infinite universe composed of countless worlds like our solar system. Anticipating Galileo Galilei, he maintained the Bible should not be the source of our cosmological thinking. He critiqued Aristotle and favored Averroes. He became ever more provocative in his theological and religious perspectives. After a brief return to Paris, Bruno moved to Germany and then, in 1590, to Venice and Padua, where he hoped to secure a chair in mathematics, which was instead offered to Galileo in 1592. In that same year, Bruno was arrested by the Venetian Inquisition and tried for his heretical positions. The Roman Inquisition then demanded his extradition and on January 27, 1593, Bruno was imprisoned in Rome for a trial that lasted seven years.

The Supreme Sacred Congregation of the Roman and Universal Inquisition demanded that Bruno retract all his theories and theological positions. Bruno finally declared that he had nothing to retract, and Pope Clement VIII ordered that he should be sentenced as an unrepentant heretic. When the death sentence was read on February 8, 1600, Bruno responded, "Perhaps your fear in passing judgment on me is greater than mine in receiving it."[5] On February 17, 1600, he was taken to the Campo de' Fiori where he was burned alive at the stake. A statue of Giordano Bruno was erected there by Freemasons in 1889.

We were told that inquisitors declared a person guilty of heresy and then handed him or her over to civil authorities for execution. In the Papal States, the pope was the civil authority. It is distressing that it did not seem to bother the "Vicar of Christ" when he approved that Bruno should be burned alive. Love was absent.

Sadly, "like all great ideas, the idea of autonomy [freedom] grounded in creation needed time before it could become part of general opinion."[6] The notion that persons retain their rights and freedom from coercion even if they are judged to be in error was finally acknowledged by article 2 of the Declaration on Religious Liberty at the Second Vatican Council. The Creator brought that kind of freedom into existence because it made the decision to love possible.

As noted above, the younger Joseph Ratzinger declared that if God, who

> upholds and encompasses everything, is consciousness, freedom, and love, then it follows automatically that the supreme factor in the world is not cosmic necessity but freedom....This leads to the conclusion that freedom is evidently the necessary structure of the world, as it were, and this again means that one can only comprehend the world as incomprehensible, that it must be incomprehensibility. For if the supreme point in the world's design is a freedom that upholds, wills, knows, and loves the whole world as freedom, then this means that together with freedom the incalculability implicit in it is an essential part of the world. Incalculability is an implication of freedom; the world can never—if this is the position—be completely reduced to mathematical logic.[7]

The Creator of such freedom and incalculability wills that the future of the world and the Church be not predetermined. Humans must decide. That requires discernment, openness to possibilities, and integrity, but above all, care for and forgiveness of one another, as emphasized in the Lord's Prayer. We must exercise our freedom with the gifts endowed by God's Spirit *present within us*: love, joy, peace, patience, kindness, goodness, faithfulness, gentleness, and self-control (Gal 5:22–23). That is "the Way" of Christians. It is likewise "the Way of every human" if they so decide.

NOTES

PREFACE

1. Kenan B. Osborne, *Ministry: Lay Ministry in the Catholic Church: Its History and Theology* (Mahwah, NJ: Paulist Press, 1993), 601.

2. Edward Schillebeeckx, *Church: The Human Story of God*, vol. 10 in The Collected Works of Edward Schillebeeckx (London: T&T Clark, Bloomsbury, 2014), 89 [91]. Brackets indicate pages in the old edition translated by John Bowden (New York: Crossroad, 1990).

3. "Dei enim verba, humanis linguis expressa, humano sermoni assimilia facta sunt." *Dei Verbum* (Dogmatic Constitution on Divine Revelation), 13, https://www.vatican.va/archive/hist_councils/ii_vatican_council/documents/vat-ii_const_19651118_dei-verbum_en.html.

4. Raymond E. Brown, "'And the Lord Said?' Biblical Reflections on Scripture as the Word of God," *Theological Studies* 42, no. 1 (1981): 3–19, at 10.

CHAPTER 1

1. David Ewing Duncan, *Calendar: Humanity's Epic Struggle to Determine a True and Accurate Year* (New York: Avon Books, 1998), 45–46.

2. Raymond E. Brown, "'And the Lord Said?'" 18.

3. Augustine, *The Literal Meaning of Genesis*, trans. and annotated by John Hammond Taylor, Ancient Christian Writers, vol. 41 (New York: Paulist Press, 1982), 19, 38.

4. Augustine, *City of God*, 16, 9.

5. In Greek, *pros ton theon*: with *the* God.

6. Karl Rahner, *Foundations of Christian Faith*, trans. William V. Dych (New York: Crossroad, 1978), 46–47.

7. Plato, *Timaeus*, 30–52.

8. See Plato, *Republic*, 507b–9b.

9. See *De Caelo*, Bk. 2, 3–14: 286a–98a 20; Bk. 1, 2 and 3: 268b 11–270b 30; Bk. 3, I: 298a 24–298b 33; *De Generatione et Corruptione*, Bk. 2, 9: 335a 24–25; *Physics*, Bk. 4, 14: 223a 29–224a 2.

10. Fraser Watts, "Darwin's Gifts to Theology," in *Theology, Evolution and the Mind*, ed. Neil Spurway (Newcastle upon Tyne: Cambridge Scholars Publishing, 2009), 53–67, at 57.

11. Joseph Ratzinger, *Introduction to Christianity*, trans. J. R. Foster and Michael J. Miller (San Francisco: Ignatius, 2004), 157–59.

12. George V. Coyne and Alessandro Omizzolo, *Wayfarers in the Cosmos: The Human Quest for Meaning* (New York: Crossroad, 2002), 168.

13. B. Wood, and M. Collard, "The Human Genus," *Science* 284 (1999): 65–71; Steven Mithen, "The Prehistory of the Religious Mind," in Spurway, *Theology, Evolution and the Mind*, 10–30.

14. I. McDougall, F. H. Brown, and J. G. Fleagle, "Stratigraphic Placement and Age of Modern Humans from Kibish, Ethiopia," *Nature* 433 (2005): 733–36; M. A. Jobling, M. E. Hurles, and C. Tyler-Smith, *Human Evolutionary Genetics* (New York: Garland, 2004).

15. B. Vandermeersch, "Une sépulture moustérienne avec offrandes découverte dans la grotte de Qafzeh," *Compte Rendus Hebdomadaires des Séances de l'Académie des Sciences* 270 (1970): 298–301; M. M. Lahr and R. Foley, "Multiple Dispersals and Modern Human Origins," *Evolutionary Anthropology* 3 (1994): 48–60.

16. M. Ingman, H. Kaessmann, S. Paabo, and U. Gyllensten, "Mitochondrial Genome Variation and the Origin of Modern Humans," *Nature* 408 (2000): 491–522; Wolfgang Haak, Iosif Lazaridis, Nick Patterson, Nadin Rohland, et al., "Massive Migration from the Steppe Was a Source for Indo-European Languages in Europe," *Nature* 522 (June 11, 2015): 207–11 used genome-wide data from sixty-nine Europeans who lived between three to eight thousand years ago to trace migrations, ancestry relationships, and language development.

17. Augustine, *City of God*, 12, 11.

18. Denis Edwards, *How God Acts: Creation, Redemption, and Special Divine Action* (Minneapolis: Fortress, 2010), 43–45.

19. Gabriel Daly, *Creation and Redemption* (Wilmington, DE: Michael Glazier, 1989), 52.

20. Schillebeeckx, *Church: The Human Story of God*, 88 [90].

21. Søren Kierkegaard, *Journals and Papers*, vol. 2: F–K, ed. and trans. Howard V. Hong and Edna H. Hong (Bloomington: Indiana University Press, 1970), 62 (no. 1251).

22. Philip Hefner, *The Human Factor: Evolution, Culture, and Religion* (Minneapolis: Fortress, 1993), 39.

23. Ilia Delio, *Christ in Evolution* (Maryknoll, NY: Orbis Books, 2008), 138.

24. Yves Congar, "Christ in the Economy of Salvation and in Our Dogmatic Tracts," *Concilium* 1, no. 2 (1966): 11.

25. Congar, "Christ in the Economy of Salvation," 11.

26. Daly, *Creation and Redemption*, 3–4.

CHAPTER 2

1. Ratzinger, *Introduction to Christianity*, 160.

2. Jacques-Bénigne Bossuet, *Discourse on Universal History*, ed. Orest Ranum, trans. Elborg Forster (Chicago: University of Chicago Press, 1976), 375.

3. Bossuet, *Discourse on Universal History*, 159.

4. Karl Löwith, *Meaning in History: The Theological Implications of the Philosophy of History* (Chicago: University of Chicago Press, 1949), 104–9.

5. Voltaire, *Candide or Optimism*, trans. Burton Raffel (New Haven: Yale University Press, 2005), 15–18 and 127.

6. Published in the January 24 and 31 issues of the *Wöchentliche Königsbergische Frag- und Anzeigungs- Nachrichten* of 1756: see Immanuel Kant, *Natural Science*, The Cambridge Edition of the Works of Immanuel Kant, ed. Eric Watkins, trans. Lewis White Beck, Jeffrey B. Edwards, Olaf Reinhardt, Martin Schönfeld, et al. (Cambridge: University of Cambridge Press, 2012), 327–36. Two later, related essays are found on pages 337–64 and 365–73.

7. John Polkinghorne, "The Laws of Nature and the Laws of Physics," in *Quantum Cosmology and the Laws of Nature: Scientific Perspectives on Divine Action*, ed. Robert John Russell, Nancey Murphy, and C. J. Isham (Vatican City: Vatican Observatory Publications; Berkeley, CA: Center for Theology and the Natural Sciences, 1993), 441.

8. Polkinghorne, "Laws of Nature," 443.

9. Polkinghorne, "Laws of Nature," 445.

10. Paul Davies, *The Cosmic Blueprint: New Discoveries in Nature's Creative Ability to Order the Universe* (New York: Simon and Schuster, 1988), 202.

11. Polkinghorne, "Laws of Nature," 446.

12. Daly, *Creation and Redemption*, 71.

13. Polkinghorne, "Laws of Nature," 447.

14. Jürgen Moltmann, "Reflections on Chaos and God's Interaction with the World from a Trinitarian Perspective," in *Chaos and Complexity: Scientific Perspectives on Divine Action*, ed. Robert John Russell, Nancey Murphy, Arthur R. Peacocke, 2nd ed. (Vatican City: Vatican Observatory Publications; Berkeley, CA: Center for Theology and the Natural Sciences, 2000), 205–10, at 209–10.

15. John Polkinghorne, "The Metaphysics of Divine Action," in Russell, *Chaos and Complexity*, 156.

16. D. J. Bartholomew, *God of Chance* (London: SCM, 1984), 82.

17. Bartholomew, *God of Chance*, 157.

18. Arthur Peacocke, *Creation and the World of Science: The Re-Shaping of Belief*, 2nd ed. (Oxford: Oxford University Press, 2004, orig. 1979), 103.

19. Arthur Peacocke, *Theology for a Scientific Age: Being and Becoming—Natural, Divine and Human* (Minneapolis: Fortress, 1993), 175.

20. Schillebeeckx, *Church: The Human Story of God*, 89 [91].

21. Elizabeth A. Johnson, "Does God Play Dice? Divine Providence and Chance," *Theological Studies* 57 (1996): 10–14; Edwards, *How God Acts*, 62–64.

22. Daly, *Creation and Redemption*, 53.

23. Alfred North Whitehead, *Process and Reality: An Essay in Cosmology* (New York: Macmillan, 1929, 6th reprint, 1967), 528.

24. Whitehead, *Process and Reality*, 522, 129–31, 46–48, 104, 248, 342–43.

25. Keith Ward, *God, Faith and the New Millennium: Christian Belief in an Age of Science* (Rockport, MA: Oneworld, 1998), 107.

26. Denis Edwards, *The God of Evolution: A Trinitarian History* (Mahwah, NJ: Paulist Press, 1999), 88–92; and Edwards, *How God Acts*, 44.

27. Ormond Rush, *Still Interpreting Vatican II: Some Hermeneutical Principles* (Mahwah, NJ: Paulist Press, 2004), 69.

28. Rush, *Still Interpreting Vatican II*, 75.

29. Rush, *Still Interpreting Vatican II*, 76.

30. Daly, *Creation and Redemption*, 43.

31. Karl Rahner, "Christology within an Evolutionary View of the World," in *Theological Investigations*, vol. 5, *Later Writings*, trans. K. H. Kruger (Baltimore: Helicon Press, 1966), 191–92.

32. Karl Rahner, "Theology and Anthropology," in *Theological Investigations*, vol. 9, *Writings of 1965–1967*, I, trans. Graham Harrison (New York: Herder and Herder, 1972), 43.

CHAPTER 3

1. Rahner, "Christology within an Evolutionary View," 159–60 and 163.

2. Rahner, "Christology within an Evolutionary View," 164–65 and 168.

3. Rahner, "Christology within an Evolutionary View," 170.

4. Rahner, "Christology within an Evolutionary View," 173.

5. Rahner, "Christology within an Evolutionary View," 174.

6. Rahner, "Christology within an Evolutionary View," 176.

7. Rahner, "Christology within an Evolutionary View," 185.

8. Rahner, "Christology within an Evolutionary View," 177–78, and Rahner, *Foundations of Christian Faith: An Introduction to the Idea of Christianity*, trans. W. V. Dych (New York, Crossroad, 1978), 197.

9. Ilia Delio, "Revisiting the Franciscan Doctrine on Christ," *Theological Studies* 64 (2003): 3–23.

10. Schillebeeckx, *Church: The Human Story of God*, 125 [126].

11. Mark 2:15–17, with the parallels in Matt 9:10–13 and Luke 5:29–32; the collection of Jesus's "Sayings" known as "Q," found in Matt 11:16–19 and Luke 7:31–34; and Luke 15.

12. *Commentary on the Epistle to the Romans*, book 2, *Solutio* (PL 178, 836).

13. Ratzinger, *Introduction to Christianity*, 282.

14. Edward Schillebeeckx, *Christ: The Christian Experience in the Modern World*, vol. 7 in The Collected Works of Edward Schillebeeckx (London: T&T Clark, Bloomsbury, 2014), 820–21 [824–25]. Brackets indicate pages in the old edition, *Christ: The Experience of Jesus as Lord*, trans. John Bowden (New York: Crossroad, 1981).

15. Schillebeeckx, *Christ*, 722 [729]

16. Ratzinger, *Introduction to Christianity*, 282–83.

17. Schillebeeckx, *Christ*, 825 [830].

18. Daly, *Creation and Redemption*, 212.

19. Walter Kasper, *The God of Jesus Christ*, trans. Matthew J. O'Connell (New York: Crossroad, 1986), 194–95.

20. Kasper, *God of Jesus Christ*, 196–97.

21. Daly, *Creation and Redemption*, 25.

CHAPTER 4

1. Justin Martyr, *First Apology* 61, in St. Justin Martyr, *The First and Second Apologies*, trans. and ed. Leslie William Barnard, vol. 56, Ancient Christian Writers (Mahwah, NJ: Paulist Press, 1997), 67.

2. Theodore de Bruyn, *Pelagius's Commentary on St. Paul's Epistle to the Romans* (Oxford: Clarendon Press, 1993), 92 and 175.

3. Augustine, *De gratia Christi (et peccato originali)*, 1, 5.

4. Augustine, *De gratia Christi*, 1, 28 and 36.

5. *De gestis Pelagii*, 20.

6. *De gestis Pelagii*, 20 and 22.

7. *De gratia Christi*, 2,14.

8. *De peccatorum meritis*, 3,14.

9. *Opus imperfectum contra Julianum*, 6, 22.

10. *De peccatorum meritis*, 2,11.

11. *De nuptiis et concupiscentia*, 1,28–29.

12. *De nuptiis et concupiscentia*, 2,57.

13. *De correptione et gratia*, 12.

14. *De correptione et gratia*, 31.

15. *Opus imperfectum contra Julianum*, 6, 22.

16. *De correptione et gratia*, 33.

17. *Against Heresies* 2,1,1. Text in *The Ante-Nicene Fathers*, vol. 1, *The Apostolic Fathers with Justin Martyr and Irenaeus*, eds. Alexander Roberts, James Donaldson, and Arthur Cleveland Coxe (New York: Cosimo Books, 2007; originally published in 1885).

18. http://www.vatican.va/archive/bible/nova_vulgata/documents/nova-vulgata_nt_epist-romanos_lt.html.

19. Rahner, *Foundations of Christian Faith*, 107.

20. Rahner, *Foundations of Christian Faith*, 111.

21. Rahner, *Foundations of Christian Faith*, 109.

22. Rahner, *Foundations of Christian Faith*, 114.

23. Daly, *Creation and Redemption*, 209.

24. Edwards, *How God Acts*, 131–34.

25. René Girard, *Things Hidden since the Foundation of the World* (Stanford, CA: Stanford University Press, 1987), 24.

26. Ernst Mayr, *What Evolution Is* (London: Weidenfeld & Nicolson, 2002), 255.

27. Edwards, *How God Acts*, 131; Mayr, *What Evolution Is*, 252.

28. Edwards, *How God Acts*, 132–33; Edward O. Wilson, *Consilience: The Unity of Knowledge* (New York: Vintage, 1998), 178–96.

29. Wilson, *Consilience*, 179.

30. Wilson, *Consilience*, 186.

31. Richard Leakey, *The Origin of Humankind* (London: Phoenix, 1994), 149 and 153–54; Edwards, *How God Acts*, 133.

32. Raymund Schwager, *Banished from Eden: Original Sin and Evolutionary Theory in the Drama of Salvation* (Leominster, UK: Gracewing, 2006), 55. Cited by Edwards, *How God Acts*, 131.

33. Mayr, *What Evolution Is*, 259; Edwards, *How God Acts*, 134.

34. *De correptione et gratia*, 12.

35. Epistle 166, 10 and 25.

36. International Theological Commission, "The Hope of Salvation for Infants Who Die without Being Baptized" (April 20, 2007), 103, http://www.vatican.va/roman_curia/congregations/cfaith/cti

_documents/rc_con_cfaith_doc_20070419_un-baptised-infants_en
.html.

37. See Rahner, *Foundations of Christian Faith*, 126–37, 178–227;
"On the Theology of the Incarnation," in *Theological Investigations*, vol.
4, *More Recent Writings*, trans. Kevin Smyth (Baltimore: Helicon, 1966),
87–117; "Jesus Christ," in *Sacramentum Mundi*, vol. 3 (New York: Herder
& Herder, 1969), 207–8; *The Trinity* (New York: Herder & Herder, 1970),
34–40, 82–103.

38. Rahner, *Foundations*, 101–2.

39. See Vatican II's Constitution on Divine Revelation (*Dei Verbum*), section 2; Kasper, *God of Jesus Christ*, 315–16.

40. James Alison, *Undergoing God: Dispatches from the Scene of a Break-In* (London: Darton Longman & Todd, 2006), 64.

41. Edwards, *How God Acts*, 138–42.

CHAPTER 5

1. John T. Noonan, *A Church That Can and Cannot Change: The Development of Catholic Moral Teaching* (Notre Dame, IN: University of Notre Dame Press, 2005).

2. Noonan, *A Church That Can and Cannot Change*, 14.

3. Noonan, *A Church That Can and Cannot Change*, 102.

4. Noonan, *A Church That Can and Cannot Change*, 87–93.

5. Noonan, *A Church That Can and Cannot Change*, 103; Immanuel Kant, *Perpetual Peace*, ed. Lewis White Beck (New York: Liberal Arts Press, 1957), sec. II, 21–23.

6. Noonan, *A Church That Can and Cannot Change*, 94.

7. Noonan, *A Church That Can and Cannot Change*, 104–8, 117.

8. Noonan, *A Church That Can and Cannot Change*, 108.

9. Noonan, *A Church That Can and Cannot Change*, 103.

10. Noonan, *A Church That Can and Cannot Change*, 116–17, 260–61.

11. Noonan, *A Church That Can and Cannot Change*, 119–23.

12. Walter Kasper, *Theology and Church*, trans. Margaret Kohl (New York: Crossroad, 1989), 59.

13. Kasper, *Theology and Church*, 60, also 36.

14. Kasper, *Theology and Church*, 62.

15. Kasper, *Theology and Church*, 63.

16. Kasper, *Theology and Church*, 68.

17. The material that follows is an updated version of Bernard P. Prusak, "Woman: Seductive Siren and Source of Sin? Pseudepigraphal Myth and Christian Origins," in *Religion and Sexism: Images of Women in the Jewish and Christian Traditions*, ed. Rosemary Ruether (New York: Simon and Schuster, 1974), 89–116.

18. "But the serpent said to the woman, 'You will not die; for God knows that when you eat of it your eyes will be opened, and you will be like God, knowing good and evil.' So when the woman saw that the tree was good for food, and that it was a delight to the eyes, and that the tree was to be desired to make one wise, she took of its fruit and ate; and she also gave some to her husband, who was with her, and he ate. Then the eyes of both were opened, and they knew that they were naked; and they sewed fig leaves together and made loincloths for themselves" (Gen 3:4–7; see also Gen 2:17).

19. *1 [Ethiopic Apocalypse of] Enoch*, E. Isaac, trans. in James H. Charlesworth, ed., *The Old Testament Pseudepigrapha*, vol.1, *Apocalyptic Literature and Testaments* (New York: Doubleday, 1983), 13–89.

20. The Watchers are "the holy angels who watch" and who do not sleep (*1 Enoch* 20:1, 39:12–13, 40:2, 61:12, 71:7). The title first appears in Daniel 4:13, 17, 23.

Compare *1 Enoch* 6:1–5 with Gen. 6:1–4, cited above:

> In those days, when the children of man had multiplied, it happened that there were born unto them handsome and beautiful daughters. And the angels, the children of heaven, saw and desired them; and they said to one another, "Come, let us choose wives for ourselves from among the daughters of man and beget us children." And Semyaz, being their leader, said unto them, "I fear that perhaps you will not consent that deed should be done, and I alone will become (responsible) for this great sin." But they all responded to him, "Let us all swear an oath and bind everyone among us by a curse not to abandon this suggestion but to do the deed."

1 Enoch 86–89 tells the entire story in symbolic dream visions written by another hand.

21. Other lists of the secrets revealed are found in 65:6–8 and 69:6–12. (As a result of the interwoven traditions, both Semyaz and Azazel are named as leaders in different passages.)

22. See *Jub.* 4:22, 5:1–11, 7:20–25. *Jubilees*, O. S. Wintermute, trans., in James H. Charlesworth, ed., *The Old Testament Pseudepigrapha*, vol. 2, *Expansions of the "Old Testament" and Legends, Wisdom and Philosophical Literature, Prayers, Psalms, and Odes, Fragments of Lost Judeo-Hellenistic Works* (Garden City, NY: Doubleday, 1985), 52–142.

23. In *Jub.* 7:21 the specific reasons for the flood are given.

24. *Jub.* 7:20–39 and 10 are probably fragments from the lost *Book of Noah* referred to in *Jub.* 10:13 and 21:10.

25. Frederick Robert Tennant, *The Sources of the Doctrine of the Fall and Original Sin* (New York: Schocken Books, 1968; orig. ed. 1903), 192, and Norman Powell Williams, *The Ideas of the Fall and of Original Sin: A Historical and Critical Study* (London and New York: Longmans, Green, 1927), 28. Note that *Jub.* 7:26–39 and 10:1–15, which attribute the post-Noachian wickedness to the demons who rose from the dying giants, are interpolations from the lost *Book of Noah.* Williams further maintains that the original author of *Jubilees* had already abandoned the Watcher legend and drew his fall story from the paradise narrative sinfulness of Adam and Eve's descendants. The Watchers are the primary causes of the corruption before the flood; the demons afterward.

26. The Watcher legend overwhelms the impact of the paradise-fall story as an explanation for the continued influence of evil.

27. *Testament of Reuben in Testaments of the Twelve Patriarchs,* trans. H. C. Kee, in Charlesworth, *Old Testament Pseudepigrapha*, vol. 1, 782–828, at 782–85.

28. References to the Watchers and their sin are also found in the *Testaments of Dan* 5:5–6 and *Naphtali* 3:5.

29. See chs. 15–30. *Apocalypse of Moses* is the title of the Greek version of the Latin *Life of Adam and Eve,* trans. M. D. Johnson, in Charlesworth, *Old Testament Pseudepigrapha*, vol. 2, 258–95.

30. Adam's account of the fall is found in *Apoc. Moses* 7:1–3 and *Life of Adam and Eve* 32–33.

31. *Apoc. Moses* 9:2, 10:2, 32:1–2; *Life of Adam and Eve* 5:3, 35:2–3, 37:2–3.

32. *2 (Slavonic Apocalypse of) Enoch*, trans. F. I. Andersen, in Charlesworth, *Old Testament Pseudepigrapha*, vol. 1, 102–213. This book is extant only in Slavonic and its date and provenance are much debated.

33. *Apocalypse of Abraham*, trans. R. Rubinkiewicz, in Charlesworth, *Old Testament Pseudepigrapha*, vol. 1, 689–705.

34. *2 (Syriac Apocalypse of) Baruch*, trans. A. F. J. Klijn, in Charlesworth, *Old Testament Pseudepigrapha*, vol. 1, 621–52. In *2 Bar.* 56:10–15, Adam is presented as in some way responsible for the Watchers' fall.

35. Sir 25:24–26. The Alexandrian Greek translation is dated after 132 BCE. The original Hebrew version was written in Palestine about 190 or 180 BCE.

36. Philo Judaeus, *Questions and Answers on Genesis*, trans. R. Markus (Cambridge, MA: Harvard University Press, 1953), Book 4:15, 288.

37. Raymond E. Brown, *The Gospel According to John*, vol. 29–29A, The Anchor Bible (Garden City, NY: Doubleday, 1986), 904–6.

38. Eusebius, *The History of the Church from Christ to Constantine*, 3:11 and 32:1–5, trans. G. A. Williamson (Minneapolis: Augsburg, 1975).

39. Another passage reflecting a positive viewpoint is the parenthesis of 1 Cor 11:11–12. Eph 5:25–30, whose Pauline authorship is disputed, is also somewhat positive in its command that husbands love their wives. Joachim Jeremias's description of the Jewish woman's position before her husband shows the uniqueness of such a command (*Jerusalem in the Time of Jesus: An Investigation into Economic and Social Conditions During the New Testament Period*, trans. F. H. Cave, et al. [Philadelphia: Fortress, 1969], 359–76).

40. Gerhard Kittel, "Die Macht auf dem Haupte I Kor. 11, 10," in *Rabbinica, Arbeiten zur Religionsgeschichte des Urchristentums*, Bd. I, Heft 3 (Leipzig: Hinrichs, 1920), 17–31. To the ancient Palestinians an uncovered head symbolized freedom. A covered head was the sign of respect for the power of another. Jewish women covered their heads by means of a complicated coiffure with plaited hair, ribbons, bands, and cloth. A bride uncovered her head as a proof of virginity. Her head was then covered to indicate that she was now placed under the husband's authority. The rabbis had a number of reasons why women should have their

heads covered: out of respect for the angels who keep the order of creation in which women were subject beings; lest evil spirits infest homes, attracted by a woman's uncovered hair. All these points are discussed in H. L. Strack and P. Billerbeck, *Kommentar zum Neuen Testament aus Talmud und Midrash*, Bd. III, *Die Briefe des Neuen Testaments und die Offenbarung Johannis* (Munich: C. H. Beck'sche Verlagsbuchhandlung, 1965; reprint of the 4th ed. 1926), 423–40.

41. Joseph A. Fitzmyer lists the proponents and discusses the problems of such an interpretation in "A Feature of Qumran Angelology and the Angels of 1 Cor 11:10," in *Paul and Qumran: Studies in New Testament Exegesis*, ed. Jerome Murphy-O'Connor (Chicago: Priory Press, 1968), 34–36. The entire article (31–47) discusses many other difficulties concerning this passage. The article was originally published in *New Testament Studies* 4, no. 1 (October 1957): 48–58.

Annie Jaubert interprets *exousia* in an active sense: it is a sign of woman's capacity and right to worship. But in actively fulfilling that obligation, Paul insists that women must conform to the order of creation where men have priority at worship. Jaubert believes that Paul renders the context positive by his observation that the two sexes are interdependent in the Lord. She suggests that 1 Cor 14:34–35 is an interpolation from the Pastorals, "Le voile des femmes (I Cor XI. 2–16)," *New Testament Studies* 18, no. 4 (July 1972): 428–30. In "Authority on Her Head: An Examination of I Cor XI. 10," *New Testament Studies* 10, no. 3 (April 1964): 410–16, M. D. Hooker likewise interprets *exousia* in an active sense: it is woman's power to reflect the glory of God in prayer and prophecy. Man is uncovered lest he who is God's image hide the glory of God. Woman is covered lest she who is from man distract the angels at worship by reflecting man's glory. Hooker feels that Paul contrived such theological reasoning to solve a practical problem at worship where men rather than angels were distracted by women's hair. God was not to be rivaled by anyone.

42. Hans Lietzmann, *An die Korinther I–II*, 4. Aufl., Bd. 9, in *Handbuch zum Neuen Testament* (Tübingen: Mohr, 1949), 55.

43. Fitzmyer, "A Feature of Qumran Angelology," 40–41.

44. Fitzmyer, "A Feature of Qumran Angelology," 41–45. See also Matthew Black, *The Scrolls and Christian Origins: Studies in the Jewish*

Background of the New Testament (London and New York: Thomas Nelson, 1961), 30.

45. Henry J. Cadbury, "A Qumran Parallel to Paul," *Harvard Theological Review* 51, no. 1 (January 1958): 1–2.

46. Annie Jaubert ("Le voile des femmes," 419) notes that the traditions to which Paul refers probably come from the more ancient churches in Palestine and Syria. To explain the requirement of head covering for women she turns to rabbinic literature (424–27). She admits that Paul's reference to the angels comes from a Jewish milieu (427–28). But the influence of the Pseudepigrapha is neglected, because Jaubert, like Fitzmyer, believes that Paul refers only to good angels who are no longer susceptible to seduction. I agree on the matter of angelic incorruptibility, but unlike Fitzmyer and Jaubert, admit a much more subtle influence of pseudepigraphal motifs. Tertullian, who is wrongly cited by Jaubert (429), as if he supported Lietzmann, does not say women must be veiled lest they again seduce the angels, but rather because they once did so. For him, the veil is a brand of shame: see *Adversus Marcionem* 5,8 and *De virginibus velandis* 7 in support of that position. Such a perspective is also found in the Midrash on Genesis, which received its final form just after the fifth century: "Why does a man go out bareheaded while a woman goes out with her head covered? She is like one who has done wrong and is ashamed of people; therefore she goes out with her head covered" (*Genesis Bereshith* 17:18, *Midrash*, I [London: Soncino Press 1961, orig ed. 1939], 139). The influence of the Watcher myth upon the Qumran community is known from the Zadokite Document (2:14–3:12); see Theodor H. Gaster, *The Dead Sea Scriptures* (New York: Anchor, 1964), 73–74.

47. See also *1 Apol.* 5:2 and *2 Apol.* 7:2ff. St. Justin Martyr, *The First and Second Apologies*, trans. and ed. Leslie William Barnard, vol. 56, Ancient Christian Writers (Mahwah, NJ: Paulist Press, 1997), 77.

48. *Dialogue with Trypho*, 100; see also 79, 124, l03 and 88. (Translation is mine.)

49. See *Adversus Haereses* 4, 36, 4; 4, 16, 2; 1, 15, 6; 5, 28, 2; *Proof of the Apostolic Preaching* 10; 18; 27 and 85 and compare with *Adv. Haer.* 5, 23, 1 and 2; 5, 16, 3; 5, 5, 1 and *Proof* 15 and 34. Chapter 18 of *Proof of the Apostolic Preaching* reads: "And wickedness very long continued and widespread pervaded all the race of men, until very little seed of justice was in them. For unlawful unions came about on earth, as angels linked

themselves with offspring of the daughters of men, who bore to them sons, who on account of their exceeding great size were called Giants. The angels, then, brought to their wives as gifts teachings of evil, for they taught them the virtues of roots and herbs, and dyeing and cosmetics and discoveries of precious materials, love-potions, hatreds, amours, passions, constraints of love, the bonds of witchcraft, every sorcery and idolatry, hateful to God; and when this was come into the world, the affairs of wickedness were propagated to overflowing, and those of justice dwindled to very little." St. Irenaeus, *Proof of the Apostolic Preaching*, trans. and ed. Joseph P. Smith, vol. 16, Ancient Christian Writers, J. Quasten and J. C. Plumpe, eds. (Westminster, MD: Newman Press, 1952), 58.

50. "[Satan] was envious of God's workmanship, and took in hand to render this [workmanship] an enmity with God" (*Adv. Haer.* 4, 40, 3). The same idea is developed in *Adv. Haer.* 5, 24,4 and *Proof* 11; 12; 16. Satan wanted man to adore him as a god (*Adv. Haer.* 5, 24, 3).

51. "For it was by means of a woman that he got the advantage over man at first, setting himself up as man's opponent'" (*Adv. Haer.* 5, 21, 1). Adam was caught in a battle between the serpent (Satan) and God. Through Jesus, God conquers Satan, restores man to His image and likeness, and recapitulates all creation (see *Adv. Haer.* 3, 16, 6; 3, 23, 1 & 2; 5, 21, 1 & 2; 4, 40, l; and *Proof* 32). Jesus the Christ placed Satan under the power of humans (*Adv. Haer.* 5, 24, 4).

52. *Adv. Haer.* 4, preface, 4; 5, 19, l; 5, 23, l; and *Proof* 16.

53. *Adv. Haer.* 3, 22, 4 and 5, 19, 1.

54. *Proof* 14; cf. *Adv. Haer.* 3, 22, 4.

55. Adam's childlike innocence is established in the following texts: *Proof* 12; 14; 16; *Adv. Haer.* 3, 22, 4; 3, 23, 5; 4, 38, 1–4; 4, 39,2. See also Theophilus of Antioch, *To Autolycus* 2, 25, and Clement of Alexandria, *Protrepticus*, 11.

56. I wish to acknowledge the many insights I received about Irenaeus from discussions with my former colleague Donald R. Schulz. His unpublished doctoral dissertation, "The Origin of Sin in Irenaeus and Jewish Apocalyptic Literature" (McMaster University, Ontario), far exceeds my analysis of Irenaeus's thinking.

57. *Adv. Haer.* 3, 23, 3 & 5: Ante-Nicene Fathers, I, 456–57.

58. *Adv. Haer.* 4, 40, 3: Ante-Nicene Fathers, I, 524.

59. See *Adv. Haer.* 5, 19, l; 5,21, l; 3,22, 4; 3,23,7; 3,21,10; and *Proof* 33.

60. *Paedagogus* 3,2 (14) in Clement of Alexandria, *Christ the Educator*, trans. Simon P. Wood, vol. 23 of The Fathers of the Church, eds. Roy Joseph Deferrari, et al. (Washington, DC: Catholic University of America Press 1954, reprinted 2008), 211. *Stromata, or Miscellanies* 5,1 in The Ante-Nicene Fathers, vol. 2, eds. Alexander Roberts, James Donaldson, and Arthur C. Coxe (New York: Cosimo Classics, 2007, orig. 1885), 446.

61. *Paedagogue* 2,12 (123); *Christ the Educator*, 195.

62. *Stromateis* 3, 17 (103); in Clement of Alexandria, *Stromateis, Books One to Three*, trans. John Ferguson, vol. 85 of The Fathers of the Church, eds. Thomas P. Halton, et al. (Washington, DC: Catholic University of America Press 1991), 321; and *Protrepticus* 11. *Exhortation to the Greeks*, in Ante-Nicene Fathers, vol. 2, 202–3.

63. *Strom.* 3, 16 (100); *Stromateis*, 319.

64. *Paed.* 2, 10 (114); *Christ the Educator*, 187–88.

65. *Paed.* 3, 11 (79); *Christ the Educator*, 259.

66. *Paed.* 2, 2 (33); *Christ the Educator*, 122–23.

67. *Paed.* 3, 3 (19); *Christ the Educator*, 214–15.

68. *In Leviticum homiliae* 12:4 and 8:3, as well as *In Lucam homiliae* 14, and *Contra Celsum* 7, 50.

69. Origen knows *1 Enoch*, but does not treat it as inspired scripture; see *De Principiis* 1, 3, 3; 4, 35 (4, 4, 8); *In Ioannem* 6:25, *Contra Celsum* 5, 54; in *Numeros homiliae* 2.8:2.

70. In *Contra Celsum* 4, 40 the curse spoken against Eve is said to apply to every woman. However, this does not seem to be especially significant, since Origen notes the same is true regarding the curse against man.

71. *De Oratione*, chs. 20–22; *De Virginibus Velandis*, chs. 4–11 (esp. ch. 7); *Adversus Marcionem*, 5, 18; and *Apologeticus* 22. To reconstruct Tertullian's demonology, compare *Apol.* 22 with *1 Enoch* 15:8–9 and *De Spectaculis*, chs. 10, 12, 13, and 23.

72. *De Virginibus Velandis* 7 (On the Veiling of Virgins), trans. S. Thelwall, in The Ante-Nicene Fathers, vol. 4, eds. Alexander Roberts James Donaldson, & Arthur C. Coxe (New York: Cosimo Classics, 2007, orig. 1885), 32.

73. *De Cultu Feminarum* 2, 10 and 1, 2 and 4 (cf. *Enoch* 8:1). In a discussion of astrology, Tertullian writes, "One proposition I lay down: that those angels, the deserters from God, the lovers of women, were likewise the discoverers of this curious art..." (*De Idololatria* 9; cf. *1 Enoch* 8:3).

74. *De Cultu Feminarum*, 1, 3; *De Idol.* 4 and 15 (cf. *1 Enoch* 19:1 and 99:6–7).

75. *De Spectaculis* 2; *De Testimonio Animae* 3; *De Carnis Resurrectione* 34; *De Carne Christi* 14.

76. *On the Apparel of Women* 1,1 (*De Cultu Feminarum*): trans. S. Thelwall, in The Ante-Nicene Fathers, vol. 4, 14.

77. *De peccatorum meritis et remissione* 1, 57; *Contra Iulianum* 5, 52 and 3, 57; *De nupt. et concup.* 1, 29 and also 20; 21; 25 and 28. For further references see J. N. D. Kelly, *Early Christian Doctrines*, 2nd ed. (New York: Harper & Row, 1960), 364–66. Perhaps Augustine reflects his friend and mentor Ambrose (see *Apol. David* 11), who in turn reflects Origen. Gregory of Nyssa in his earlier *De Opificio hominis*, 16–17, held that all sexual distinction and generation originated from the Fall (see also *De Virginitate* 3). He retreated from that position in his later *Catechetical Oration*.

78. Canon 813 § 1. *Sacerdos Missam ne celebret sine ministro, qui eidem inserviat et respondeat. § 2. Minister Missam inserviens ne sit mulier, nisi, deficiente viro, justa de causa, eaque lege ut mulier ex longinquo respondeat nec ullo pacto ad altare accedat.*

79. AAS 41, 2 (1949), 493–511, at 507–8:4. *Exceptis necessitatis casibus in n. 2 enumeratis, vi citati can. 813 requiritur praesentia ministri in Missae celebratione : rubrica missalis praefert, quantum fieri possit, clericum laico, qui est adhibendus si clericus desit, qui et ipse debet esse masculini sexus : **omnes AA. unanimiter docent esse sub mortali prohibitum mulieribus, etiamsi moniales sint, ministrare ad altare.** Sapienter igitur Ecclesia prioribus temporibus statuerat esse adhi bendum qua ministrum in Missa privata clericum prima tonsura insignitum (S. R. O., Coli. auth. decr., decr. 113, ad VI) ; et solum temporum decursu, clericis pro tali servitio rarefactis, ex necessitate concessit ut laici adhiberentur praesertim pueri (ibi, decr. 3847, ad VII) : qui usus hodie latissime patet. Ad pueros quod attinet, hi debent sedulo institui ut idonei fiant administri huic pernobili muneri explendo.*

5. *Casu necessitatis, deficiente viro, clerico aut laico, rei. canon 813 mulierem admittit ad servitium s. Missae, sub conditione tamen ut « ex longiquo respondeat, nec ullo pacto ad altare accedat ». Id etiam valebat iure Decretalium,12 ubi legitur « prohibendum quoque est, ut nulla foemina ad altare praesumat accedere aut presbytero ministrare aut intra cancellos stare sive sedere » : mulieris igitur ministerium ad hoc reducitur ut celebranti /respondeat:13* proinde oportet ut ante Missam omnia sacerdoti commode disponantur quae divino Sacrificio occurrere possint, uti solet fieri in cappellis monialium, cum desit minister. Ut mulier adhibeatur loco ministri masculini sexus, iuxta relati canonis praescriptum requiritur iusta causa. Indultis vero, quae conceduntur ab hac S. Congregatione, litandi sine ministro, clausula semper adiicitur cavendi nempe «ut ad mentem can. 813, nedum pueri edoceantur de modo inserviendi s. Missae sed etiam fideles, ipsaeque mulieres addiscant quomodo possint Missae inservire, legendo responsiones sacerdoti celebranti reddendas». Nuper vero Sanctitas Sua aliam clausulam indulto litandi Missam sine ministro inserendam praecepit, nempe «dummodo aliquis fidelis Sacro assistat», cui nullimode derogari praestat. http://www.vatican.va/archive/aas/documents/AAS-41-1949-ocr.pdf.

80. https://www.vatican.va/content/francesco/en/motu_proprio/documents/papa-francesco-motu-proprio-20210110_spiritus-domini.html.

CHAPTER 6

1. Raymond E. Brown, *The Community of the Beloved Disciple* (New York: Paulist Press, 1979), 84–88.

2. Bernard P. Prusak, *The Church Unfinished: Ecclesiology through the Centuries* (Mahwah, NJ: Paulist Press, 2004), 162–64.

3. Epistle 31.9: *Patrologia Latina* (hereafter *PL*), 33, 121–25.

4. Epistle 25.5, *PL*, 33, 101–3.

5. "Mulieres vero fugas sicut serpemtes, et numquam loquaris cum aliqua nisi urgens necessitas te compellat, nec usquam aspicias in faciem alicujus mulieris; et si mulier tecum loquatur, verba sua citissime occide." S. Bonaventurae Eximii Ecclesiae Doctoris, Opusculum, *Regula*

Novitiorum, XI. S. Bonaventurae, *Praestantissima Opuscula* (Mechliniae: H. Dessain, 1892), 151–52.

6. James R. Cain, *The Influence of the Cloister on the Apostolate of Congregations of Religious Women* (Rome: Pontificia Università Lateranensis, 1965), 6.

7. Cain, *Influence of Cloister*, 14–35.

8. Cain, *Influence of Cloister*, 37–50.

9. J. Grisar, "Die Ersten Anklagen im Rom Gegen Das Institut Maria Wards," in *Miscellanea Historiae Pontificiae in Pontificia Universitate Gregoriana*, XXII (Rome: Gregorian University, 1959), 203–4; cited by Cain, *Influence of the Cloister*, 42.

10. Cain, *Influence of the Cloister*, 48–58.

11. Carmel McEnroy, *Guests in Their Own House: The Women of Vatican II* (New York: Crossroad, 1996).

12. "Commentary on the Declaration of the Sacred Congregation for the Doctrine of the Faith on the Question of Admission of Women to the Ministerial Priesthood," in *Women Priests: A Catholic Commentary on the Vatican Declaration*, eds. Leonard Swidler and Arlene Swidler (New York: Paulist Press, 1977), 319–37, at 319. The mimeographed and unsigned Commentary was issued simultaneously with the Declaration.

13. "Commentary on the Declaration," 310–20.

14. See the Report of the Pontifical Biblical Commission on the question of the ordination of women to the ministerial priesthood in *Origins* 6, no.6, 92–96. Also in *Women Priests*, 37–49.

15. John R. Donahue, "A Tale of Two Documents," in *Women Priests*, 25.

16. http://www.vatican.va/roman_curia/congregations/cfaith/documents/rc_con_cfaith_doc_19761015_inter-insigniores_en.html. "Declaratio circa quaestionem admissionis mulierum ad sacerdotium ministeriale" (*Inter Insigniores*), *AAS* 69 (1997), 98–116. English translation in *Women Priests*, 37–49.

17. See Bernard P. Prusak, "Use the Other Door; Stand at the End of the Line," in *Women Priests*, 81–84.

18. Raymond E. Brown, "*Episkopē* and *Episkopos*: The New Testament Evidence," *Theological Studies* 41, no. 2 (1980): 323–24 and n. 4.

19. Cyprian, *Ep.* 55.17.

20. *Ep.* 27.1–2.

21. *Apostolic Tradition*, Church Order (3rd century, Rome?).

22. Cyprian, *Ep.* 23.

23. *Ep.* 15.1.2.

24. *Ep.* 38.1.2, 2.1; 39.2, 4.2.

25. *Ep.* 57.3.2: "episcopatus nostri honor grandis est…pacem dedisse martyribus."

26. *Ep.* 49.2.4.

27. Allen Brent, "Cyprian's Reconstruction of the Martyr Tradition," *Journal of Ecclesiastical History* 53, no. 2 (2002): 241–68, at 266–67.

28. Cyprian, *Ep.* 63.14.4: "Si Christus Jesus Dominus et Deus noster ipse est summus sacerdos Dei Patris, et sacrificium Patrri se ipsum obtulit, et hoc fieri in sui commemorationem praecepit, utique ille sacerdos vice Christi vere fungitur, qui id quod Christus fecit imitatur et sacrifium verum et plenum tunc offert in ecclesia Deo Patri, si sic incipiat offerre secundum quod Christum videat obtulisse"; see John D. Laurance, *Priest as Type of Christ: The Leader of the Eucharist in Salvation History according to Cyprian of Carthage* (New York: Peter Lang, 1984), 224–25.

29. Ignatius of Antioch, *Ep. Smyrnaeans* 8, *Magnesians* 6; *Trallians* 3.

30. Book 5, 1, 41.

31. Brent, "Cyprian's Reconstruction of the Martyr Tradition," 257. Brent attributes that comment to Stuart G. Hall, "Women among the Early Martyrs," in *Martyrs and Martyrologies*, ed. Diane Wood, Studies in Church History 30 (Oxford: Blackwell, 1993), 21.

32. *Ep.* 63.14.4.

33. Karl Rahner, "Women and the Priesthood," in *Theological Investigations*, vol. 20, *Concern for the Church*, trans. Edward Quinn (New York: Crossroad, 1981), 35–47.

34. Rahner, "Women and the Priesthood," 35.

35. Rahner, "Women and the Priesthood," 37.

36. Rahner, "Women and the Priesthood," 38–39.

37. Rahner, "Women and the Priesthood," 39.

38. Rahner, "Women and the Priesthood," 39–40.

39. Rahner, "Women and the Priesthood," 40.

40. Rahner, "Women and the Priesthood," 41.

41. Rahner, "Women and the Priesthood," 42–43.

42. Rahner, "Women and the Priesthood," 43.

43. Rahner, "Women and the Priesthood," 47.

44. http://w2.vatican.va/content/john-paul-ii/en/apost_letters/ 1994/documents/hf_jp-ii_apl_19940522_ordinatio-sacerdotalis.html.

45. Rahner, "Women and the Priesthood," 41.

46. Mansi 52, 1226–27; see Gustave Thils, *L'Infaillibilité pontificale: source—conditions—limites* (Gembloux: Éditions J. Duculot, 1969), 245–51, see also 161 and 207–9; Francis A. Sullivan, *Magisterium: Teaching Authority in the Catholic Church* (Mahwah, NJ: Paulist Press, 1983), 133 & 140; and "Note: The 'Secondary Object' of Infallibility," in *Theological Studies* 54 (1993): 538–39 and 544.

47. For the Latin texts of the drafts in parallel columns, see Jean-Pierre Torrell, *La théologie de l'épiscopat au Premier Concile du Vatican* (Paris: Cerf, 1961), 313.

48. See Thils, *L'infaillibilité pontificale*, 162–63.

49. "Responsio ad dubium circa doctrinam in Epist. Ap. 'Ordinatio Sacerdotalis' traditam," *Acta Apostolicae Sedis* 87, no. 12 (1995): 1114, http://www.vatican.va/roman_curia/congregations/cfaith/documents/rc _con_cfaith_doc_19951028_dubium-ordinatio-sac_lt.html.

50. Vatican Press Office, Bulletin: "The Pope Speaks with Journalists on the Return Flight from Sweden," November 2, 2016, https://press .vatican.va/content/salastampa/en/bollettino/pubblico/2016/11/02/ 161102a.html.

51. Joshua J. McElwee, "Pope Francis Confirms Finality of Ban on Ordaining Women Priests," *National Catholic Reporter*, November 1, 2016, https://www.ncronline.org/news/vatican/pope-francis-confirms -finality-ban-ordaining-women.

52. Rahner, "Women and the Priesthood," 45–47.

53. Avery Dulles, "*Ius Divinum* as an Ecumenical Problem," in *A Church to Believe In: Discipleship and the Dynamics of Freedom* (New York: Crossroad, 1982), 102. (Originally published in *Theological Studies*, vol. 18, no. 4, 681–708).

54. https://blogs.loc.gov/law/2021/04/50-years-of-womens -suffrage-in-switzerland/.

55. Ratzinger, *Introduction to Christianity*, 157–59.

56. *Summa Theologiae* 3, q. 9, a. 1–4.

57. *Summa Theologiae* 3, q. 10, a. 2, resp.; cited from the translation by Fathers of the English Dominican Province, *Summa Theologica*, vol. 2 (New York: Benziger Brothers, 1947), 2087.

58. https://www.vatican.va/roman_curia/congregations/cfaith/cti_documents/rc_cti_1985_coscienza-gesu_en.html.

59. Raymond Moloney, *The Knowledge of Christ* (London: Continuum, 1999), 124.

60. Karl Rahner, "Dogmatic Reflections on the Knowledge and Self-Consciousness of Christ," *Theological Investigations*, vol. 5, trans. Karl-H. Kruger (London: Darton Longman and Todd; Baltimore: Helicon, 1966), 193–215; Edward Schillebeeckx, *Jesus: An Experiment in Christology*, trans. Hubert Hoskins (New York: Crossroad, 1995), 256–71; Moloney, *The Knowledge of Christ*, 82–138.

61. Karl Rahner, "Aspects of the Episcopal Office," *Theological Investigations*, vol. 14 (New York: Seabury, 1976), 187.

62. Karl Rahner, "The Provenance of the Church in the History of Salvation from the Death and Resurrection of Jesus," in Karl Rahner and Wilhelm Thüsing, *A New Christology*, trans. David Smith and Verdant Green (New York: Seabury, 1980), 26.

63. Rush, *Still Interpreting Vatican II*, 79.

64. John O'Malley, "Reform, Historical Consciousness and Vatican II's *Aggiornamento*," *Theological Studies* 32 (1971): 573–601, at 597.

65. Karl Rahner, "A Fragmentary Aspect of a Theological Evaluation of the Concept of the Future," in *Theological Investigations*, vol. 10, *Writings of 1965–67 II*, trans. David Bourke (New York: Herder and Herder, 1973), 237.

66. Karl Rahner, *Foundations of Christian Faith: An Introduction to the Ideal of Christianity*, trans. William V. Dych (New York: Seabury, 1978), 459.

CHAPTER 7

1. Karl Rahner, "How the Priest Should View His Official Ministry," *Theological Investigations*, vol. 14, *Ecclesiology, Questions in the Church, the Church in the World*, trans. David Bourke (New York: Seabury, 1976), 207.

2. John D. Zizioulas, *Being as Communion: Studies in Personhood and the Church* (Crestwood, NY: St. Vladimir's Seminary Press, 1985), 215–16.

3. In n. 19, Zizioulas refers to *1 Clement* 40, 3 as implying a specifically defined order, which is not to be confused with other orders.

4. Kenan B. Osborne, *Ministry: Lay Ministry in the Roman Catholic Church, Its History and Theology* (Mahwah, NJ: Paulist Press, 1993), 608.

5. Clifford Howell, SJ, "From Trent to Vatican II," in *The Study of Liturgy*, rev. ed., ed. Cheslyn Jones, Geoffrey Wainwright, Edward Yarnold, SJ, and Paul Bradshaw (New York: Oxford University Press, 1992), 287.

6. Ch. 2, section 21, http://www.intratext.com/IXT/ENG0012/_PC.HTM.

7. Ch. 2, 43: https://www.vatican.va/roman_curia/congregations/ccdds/documents/rc_con_ccdds_doc_20030317_ordinamento-messale_en.html. "In the dioceses of Canada, the faithful should kneel at the Consecration, except when prevented on occasion by ill health, or for reasons of lack of space, of the large number of people present, or for another reasonable cause. However, those who do not kneel ought to make a profound bow when the Priest genuflects after the Consecration. Where it is the practice for the people to remain kneeling after the Sanctus (Holy, Holy, Holy) until the end of the Eucharistic Prayer and before Communion when the Priest says Ecce Agnus Dei (This is the Lamb of God), it is laudable for this practice to be retained."

8. Michael Sean Winters, "People Seize on McCarrick Laicization for Their Own Agendas," *National Catholic Reporter*, February19, 2019, https://www.ncronline.org/news/opinion/distinctly-catholic/people-seize-mccarrick-laicization-their-own-agendas.

9. Walbert Bühlmann, *The Coming of the Third Church: An Analysis of the Present and Future of the Church* (Maryknoll, NY: Orbis, l977), 248–60.

10. Bühlmann, *Coming of the Third Church*, 253.

11. Center for Applied Research in the Apostolate (CARA), "Frequently Requested Church Statistics": http://cara.georgetown.edu/frequently-requested-church-statistics/.

12. Practical Provisions, Article 1: http://www.vatican.va/roman
_curia/congregations/cclergy/documents/rc_con_interdic_doc_150
81997_en.html.

13. Committee on the Laity of the United States Conference of
Catholic Bishops (USCCB), *Co-Workers in the Vineyard of the Lord*. It
was approved by the full body of bishops at its November 2005 General
Meeting as a resource for guiding the development of lay ecclesial ministry in the Catholic Church in the United States, https://cdn.ymaws.com/
www.nalm.org/resource/resmgr/documents/coworkers/co-workers_in
_the_vineyard_o.pdf.

14. USCCB, *Co-Workers*, 22–23; John Paul II, *Pastores Gregis* (On
the Bishop, Servant of the Gospel of Jesus Christ for the Hope of the
World) (Vatican City, 2003), no. 26: http://www.vatican.va/holy_father/
john_paul_ii/apost_exhortations/documents/hf_jp-ii_exh_20031016
_pastores-gregis_en.html.

15. USCCB, *Co-Workers*, 24; *Lumen Gentium* 10.

16. Osborne, *Ministry*, 552.

17. Leo Cunibert Mohlberg, ed., *Missale Francorum*, Rerum Ecclesiasticarum Documenta, Series Maior, Fontes II (Rome: Herder, 1957),
10.

18. P. Jounel, "Ordinations" in *The Church at Prayer*, vol. 3, *The
Sacraments*, ed. A. G. Martimort, trans. Matthew J. O'Connell (Collegeville, MN: Liturgical Press, 1987), 164.

19. The sermons and epistles of Pope Leo are found in *PL* 54.

20. Kissing the pope's foot was a practice that survived beyond
1925: "It is well known that the Pope wears for everyday shoes, red, thin-
soled, flat-heeled slippers, made of cloth or silk, according to the season.
On the vamp of these shoes a gold cross is embroidered, which faithful
Catholics, admitted to a private audience, kiss after having made three
genuflections, according to etiquette." John Abel Nainfa, *Costume of Prel-
ates of the Catholic Church* (Baltimore: John Murphy, 1926), 124.

21. Text in *Readings in Church History*, vol. 1, *From Pentecost to
the Protestant Revolt*, ed. Colman J. Barry (Westminster, MD: Newman
Press, 1960), 326.

22. Sermons 2 and 3, "*In Consecratione Pontificis Maximi*" (*PL*
217, 658, and 665).

23. *Register* 1.326; *PL* 214,292). For a review of the literature about this title, see Yves Congar, "Titres donnés au pape," reprinted from *Concilium* 108 (Tours, 1975) in *Droit ancien et structures ecclésiales* (London: Variorum Reprints, 1982), VI, 61.

24. Sermon 2 (*PL* 217, 658).

25. *Register* 1.485: *Cum inter alios*; 3.44 (*PL* 214, 453 and 931–32).

26. Osborne, *Ministry*, 580–81.

27. Paul F. Bradshaw, *Rites of Ordination: Their History and Theology* (Collegeville, MN: Liturgical Press, 2013), 44.

28. Gabriel Daly, *Creation and Redemption* (Wilmington, DE: Michael Glazier, 1989), 210.

29. Joseph A. Fitzmyer, *The Gospel According to Luke X–XXIV: Introduction, Translation, and Notes*, Anchor Bible 28a (New York: Doubleday, 1985), 1393–94.

30. Fitzmyer, *Gospel According to Luke*, 1399–400.

31. Fitzmyer, *Gospel According to Luke*, 1399.

32. Richard J. Dillon, "Acts of the Apostles," in *The New Jerome Biblical Commentary*, ed. R. E. Brown, J. A. Fitzmyer, and R. E. Murphy (Englewood Cliffs, NJ: Prentice-Hall, 1990), 724–25; Gerhard A. Krodel, *Acts*, Augsburg Commentary on the New Testament (Minneapolis, MN: Augsburg, 1986), 14–18, 375–79; Ernst Haenchen, *The Acts of the Apostles: A Commentary* (Philadelphia: Westminster, 1971), 60–71, 90–110; Richard J. Dillon and Joseph A. Fitzmyer, "Acts of the Apostles," in *The Jerome Biblical Commentary*, ed. R. E. Brown, J. A. Fitzmyer, and R. E. Murphy (Englewood Cliffs, NJ: Prentice-Hall, 1968), vol. 2, 166–67.

33. Raymond E. Brown, *Priest and Bishop: Biblical Reflections* (New York: Paulist Press, 1970), 41, 55; *The Critical Meaning of the Bible* (New York: Paulist Press, 1981), 77–78; *Biblical Exegesis and Church Doctrine* (New York: Paulist Press, 1985), 47–48; Jean Delorme, "Diversité et unité des ministères d'après le Nouveau Testament," in *Le ministère et les ministères selon le Nouveau Testament: dossier exégétique et réflexion théologique*, ed. J. Delorme (Paris: Éditions du Seuil, 1974), 308–9.

34. William R. Schoedel, *Ignatius of Antioch: A Commentary on the Letters of Ignatius of Antioch* (Philadelphia: Fortress, 1985), 244. See James F. McCue, "Bishops, Presbyters, and Priests in Ignatius of Antioch," *Theological Studies* 28 (1967): 828–34.

35. Alexandre Faivre, *The Emergence of the Laity in the Early Church*, trans. David Smith (Mahwah, NJ: Paulist Press, 1990), 5–40.

36. Faivre, *Emergence of Laity*, 40.

37. See Norbert Brox, *A Concise History of the Early Church*, trans. John Bowden (New York: Continuum, 1995), 116–17.

38. Robert Daly, *The Origins of the Christian Doctrine of Sacrifice* (Philadelphia: Fortress, 1978), 133–34.

39. Edward Foley, *From Age to Age: How Christians Have Celebrated the Eucharist*, rev. and expanded edition (Collegeville, MN: Liturgical Press, 2008), 68.

40. Sermon 227; cited by Foley, *From Age to Age*, 120.

41. Tertullian, "Differentiam inter ordinem et plebem constituit Ecclesiae auctoritas," *De exhortatione castitatis*, 7, 3 (CCL 2, 1024–25).

42. *Apostolic Tradition*, in Geoffrey J. Cuming, *Hippolytus: A Text for Students* (Bramcote, UK: Grove Books, 1976; 2nd ed. 1987).

43. Faivre, *Emergence of Laity*, 74–82; *Naissance d'une hiérarchie: les premières étapes du cursus clérical* (Paris: Beauchesne, 1977), 49–50.

44. Paul F. Bradshaw, *Ordination Rites of the Ancient Churches of East and West* (New York: Pueblo, 1990), Canon 2, 110.

45. Peter Brown, *Through the Eye of a Needle: Wealth, the Fall of Rome, and the Making of Christianity in the West, 350–550 AD* (Princeton, NJ: Princeton University Press, 2012), 241.

46. Brown, *Through the Eye of a Needle*, 243.

47. Brown, *Through the Eye of a Needle*, 244.

48. Teresa Berger, *Women's Ways of Worship: Gender Analysis and Liturgical History* (Collegeville, MN: Liturgical Press, 1999), 47.

49. *Apostolic Constitutions*, 2.57.3–7.

50. Peter Brown, *The Body and Society: Men, Women, and Sexual Renunciation in Early Christianity* (New York: Columbia University Press, 1988), 138–39.

51. Brown, *Body and Society*, 359–61. See Ambrose, *De Virginibus* 1.3–7 and Pope Siricius, *Ep.* 1.10,14, which refers to the unmarried clerical state as "better."

52. Brown, *Body and Society*, 426–27.

53. *Against the Epistle of Parmenian* 2.8.15–16.

54. Brown, *Body and Society*, 410, 435, 248–49.

55. Brown, *Body and Society*, 431–32; Suzanne F. Wemple, *Women in Frankish Society: Marriage and the Cloister, 500 to 900* (Philadelphia: University of Pennsylvania Press, 1981), 134–35. The Eastern churches adopted a different stance and allowed deacons and priests to continue in their marriages. They were to abstain from sexual relations when they had to celebrate the divine services.

56. Richard W. Southern, *Western Society and the Church in the Middle Ages* (London: Penguin, 1970, 1990 reprint), 340–41.

57. See Pope Siricius, *Ep.* 1.10,14; First Council of Orange (441), canon 22; Second Synod of Arles (443), canons 2 and 55; Synod at Agde or Languedoc (506), canon 16.

58. *On Divine Names* 3.1; 4.2 and 6–10; 5.3; 6.1; 8.2.

59. *Heav. Hier.* 3.1; *Eccl. Hier.* 1.3.

60. *Heav Hier.* 6; *Eccl. Hier.* 5.1,1–2.

61. *Eccl. Hier.* 5.3,7, which explains the bishop's role as teacher or illuminator; cf. 5.1,7 and 5.2; *Heav. Hier.* 1.1–2 and also *Apostolic Constitutions* 8.4.6.

62. The triad of three orders is described in *Eccl. Hier.* 5.1,4–7. The bishop is called the "head of the hierarchical order." See 1.3; 5.1,5; and 7.3,7.

63. *Eccl. Hier.*, chs. 2–4.

64. *Eccl. Hier.*, 6.1,1–3.

65. *Eccl. Hier.*, 5.1,3; 6.3,5.

66. Walter Kasper, *Theology and Church* (New York: Crossroad, 1989), 62.

67. Foley, *From Age to Age*, 87.

68. Foley, *From Age to Age*, 143.

69. Foley, *From Age to Age*, 157.

70. Foley, *From Age to Age*, 178. Leo Cunibert Mohlberg, ed., *Missale Francorum*, Rerum Ecclesiasticarum Documenta, Sereis Maior, Fontes II (Rome: Herder, 1957), 10: Consecratio Manus. Consecrentur manus istae et sanctificentur per istam unctionem et nostram benedictionem, ut quaecumque benedixerint benedicta sint, et quaecumque sanctificaverint sanctificcentur. Per dominum.

71. Foley, *From Age to Age*, 167.

72. Foley, *From Age to Age*, 168.

73. Foley, *From Age to Age*, 171.

74. Foley, *From Age to Age*, 125.

75. Foley, *From Age to Age*, 125–28.

76. Foley, *From Age to Age*, 128.

77. See Pierre J. Payer, *Sex and the Penitentials: The Development of a Sexual Code, 550–1150* (Toronto: University of Toronto Press, 1984), 24–25.

78. Osborne, *Ministry*, 326.

79. Osborne, *Ministry*, 327.

80. Jean de Montclos, *Lanfranc et Bérengar: La controverse eucharistique du XIe siècle* (Leuven: Spicilegium Sacrum Lovaniense, 1971), 88, 123–24, 184–85.

81. Joseph Jungmann, *The Mass of the Roman Rite, Its Origins and Development*, rev. and abr. edition (New York: Benziger, 1959), 90, 92, 425–26; E. Dumoutet, *Le désir de voir l'hostie et les origines de la dévotion au Saint-Sacrement* (Paris: Beauchesne, 1926); and V. L. Kennedy, "The Moment of Consecration and the Elevation of the Host," *Medieval Studies* 6 (1944): 121–50.

82. The elevation of the cup began only at the end of the thirteenth century. Since the faithful could not see the species of wine in the cup, the eucharist in that form was not venerated as intensely as the host.

83. *Summa Theologiae* 3, q. 80, a. 10; Council of Trent, session 22, ch. 6, in *Decrees of the Ecumenical Councils*, vol. 2, *Trent to Vatican II*, ed. Norman P. Tanner (Washington, DC: Georgetown University Press, 1990), 734.

84. See, for example, Iosepho A. de Aldama, "De Actione Sacrificali Sacrificii Eucharistici," in *Sacrae Theologiae Summa IV* (Madrid: Biblioteca de Autores Cristianos, 1956), 337.

85. Foley, *From Age to Age*, 225.

86. See Tanner, *Decrees of the Ecumenical Councils*, vol. 1, *Nicaea to Lateran V*, 418–19.

87. "The Ninety-Five Theses," in *Martin Luther*, ed. John Dillenberger (Garden City, NY: Anchor Books, 1961), 490–500.

88. Martin Luther, "To the Christian Nobility of the German Nation," trans. Charles M. Jacobs, rev. James Atkinson, in *Three Treatises* (Philadelphia: Fortress, 1970), 12.

89. Luther, "To the Christian Nobility," 12.

90. Martin Luther, "The Babylonian Captivity of the Church," trans. A. T. W. Steinhäuser, rev. C. Ahrens and Abdel Ross Wentz, in *Three Treatises* (Philadelphia: Fortress, 1970), 244–45.

91. Luther, "Babylonian Captivity," 245.

92. "Babylonian Captivity," 247.

93. Martin Luther, *Commentary on Psalm 82*, article 4, in *Luther's Works*, vol. 13, *Selected Psalms II*, ed. Jaroslav Pelikan (St. Louis: Concordia, 1956), 65.

94. Foley, *From Age to Age*, 249–51; James F. White, *Roman Catholic Worship: Trent to Today*, 2nd ed. (Collegeville, MN: Pueblo, 2003), 2–3, 26–28.

95. Foley, *From Age to Age*, 250.

96. Howell, "From Trent to Vatican II," 287.

97. Theodore Klauser, *A Short History of the Western Liturgy*, 2nd ed., trans. John Halliburton (New York: Oxford University Press, 1979), 117–23.

98. Howell, "From Trent to Vatican II," 288.

99. Howell, "From Trent to Vatican II," 289.

100. *Institutions liturgiques*, 2nd ed. (Paris: Société Genérale de Librairie Catholique, 1878), tome 2, 12–13.

101. *Institutions liturgiques*, 16.

102. *AAS* 36 (1903), 329–39; "The Restoration of Church Music," in R. Kevin Seasoltz, *The New Liturgy: A Documentation, 1903–1965* (New York: Herder and Herder, 1966), 5–6.

103. *AAS* 38 (1905), 400–406; "The Daily Reception of Holy Communion," in Seasoltz, *New Liturgy*, 11–15.

104. White, *Roman Catholic Worship*, 81.

105. Sonya A. Quitslund, *Beauduin: A Prophet Vindicated* (New York: Newman Press), 1973, 22–24.

106. Howell, "From Trent to Vatican II," 290; Lambert Beauduin, *Liturgy the Life of the Church*, trans. Virgil Michel (Collegeville, MN: Liturgical Press, 1926).

107. Quitslund, *Beauduin*, 206.

108. English translation from http://www.vatican.va/holy_father/pius_xii/encyclicals/documents/hf_p-xii_enc_20111947_mediator-dei_en.html.

109. C. Vagaggini, "Idee fondamentali della Costituzione," in *La Sacra Liturgia rinnovata dal Concilio*, ed. G. Barauna (Turin: Elle Di Ci, 1965), 62–63.

110. Cyprian, *On the Unity of the Catholic Church*, 7; *Epistle* 66, 8, 3.

111. Aloys Grillmeier, "The Mystery of the Church," in *Commentary on the Documents of Vatican II*, vol. 1, ed. Herbert Vorgrimler (New York: Herder and Herder, 1967), 146.

112. Grillmeier, "Mystery of the Church," 157–58.

113. https://www.vatican.va/content/francesco/en/speeches/2018/october/documents/papa-francesco_20181003_apertura-sinodo.html.

114. CARA, "Frequently Requested Church Statistics," http://cara.georgetown.edu/frequently-requested-church-statistics/.

CHAPTER 8

1. Matt 13:36–43; see W. F. Albright and C. S. Mann, *Matthew*, The Anchor Bible, eds. W. F. Albright and D. N. Freedman (Garden City, NY: Doubleday, 1971), 306–10.

2. Acts 9:2; 19:9, 23; 22:4; 24:14, 22. The Way of the Lord: Acts 18:25; the Way of God: Acts 18:26.

3. Edward Schillebeeckx, *Church: The Human Story of God* (London: Bloomsbury, 2014), 123–24 [124–25].

4. Schillebeeckx, *Church: The Human Story of God*, 119 [120].

5. https://www.britannica.com/biography/Giordano-Bruno.

6. Kasper, *Theology and Church*, 60.

7. Ratzinger, *Introduction to Christianity*, 157–59.

INDEX

181

Index